How To Read Music

THIS IS A CARLTON BOOK

Copyright © Carlton Books Limited 1999

First published in 1999 by Carlton Books Limited

10 9 8 7 6 5 4 3 2 1

A CIP catalogue record for this book is available from
the British Library

ISBN 1 85868 657 1

Project Editor: Lucian Randall
Music Consultant: Andrew O'Brien
Design Manager: Zoë Mercer
Edited and designed by Terry Burrows
Production: Alexia Turner
CD recorded at the Piano Factory, London and produced
by The Orgone Company.

Printed and bound in Dubai

TERRY BURROWS

How To Read Music

READING MUSIC
MADE SIMPLE

CARLTON

Contents

FOREWORD

A Few Words...

For most adults, learning how to read music is rather like learning a language that uses an unfamiliar alphabet. Westerners encountering Russian or Japanese for the first time may be able to pick up some basic phrases within a few days, but the skill of being able to recognize those words when they are written down inevitably takes much longer to acquire.

WHAT'S IT ALL ABOUT?

The discrepancy between oral and visual learning described above deters many "illiterate" musicians from ever learning how to read music. Those with a background of classical tuition will ideally have learned to play an instrument and read music at the same time, both skills developing side-by-side. However, for the competent self-taught musician, going back to basics can easily seem like unduly hard work. And yet you may be surprised how quickly it is possible to achieve excellent results by putting in little more than a few hours work each week.

How To Read Music is a self-contained audio-visual tutor. Throughout the course of the ten lessons, you will learn the basics of sight reading as well as the general principles of music theory. Lessons are arranged so that new ideas of increasing complexity are systematically introduced. These are reinforced by frequent reading and listening exercises. By the time you complete the course you should find that you are equipped with enough knowledge to work your way through some of the most demanding pieces of music.

The book is an ideal primer for musicians of every level, from the complete novice to the expert player who has never learned about music theory, or who has simply erased those music lessons that many of us painfully had to endure during childhood. The course

SIGHT AND SOUND
∽∽∽∽

THROUGHOUT THE COURSE, NEW LESSONS ARE REINFORCED BY A SERIES OF LISTENING AND READING TESTS. WHEREVER YOU SEE A SHADED BOX THAT CONTAINS THE "EAR" SYMBOL YOU WILL BE ASKED TO ANSWER A SERIES OF QUESTIONS BASED ON SPECIFIC TRACKS ON THE CD.

SIMILARLY, A BOX THAT CONTAINS THE "EYE" SYMBOL INDICATES EITHER A PERFORMANCE OR READING TEST. IN SUCH CASES YOU WILL BE ASKED TO LOOK AT A PIECE OF MUSIC AND EITHER IDENTIFY ASPECTS OF THE NOTATION, OR ALTERNATIVELY, SING OR PLAY THE EXAMPLE ON YOUR CHOSEN INSTRUMENT. YOU CAN CHECK THAT YOU HAVE ANSWERED CORRECTLY BY LISTENING TO THE CD.

HOW TO USE THE CD

∞∞∞∞

HOW TO READ MUSIC ALSO INCLUDES A 70-MINUTE COMPACT DISC. ITS CONTENTS CAN BE GROUPED INTO TWO CATEGORIES. THE FIRST IS TO PROVIDE AURAL REINFORCEMENT OF NEW CONCEPTS OR EXAMPLES. FOR EXAMPLE, IF YOU SEE A PIECE OF MUSIC CONTAINING A STRING OF NOTES YOU WILL BE ABLE TO HEAR EXACTLY WHAT IT SOUNDS LIKE, THUS FORGING AN IMMEDIATE LINK BETWEEN THE NOTATION AND THE MUSIC. THIS RECOGNITION OF NOTE AND RHYTHM PATTERNS IS CRUCIAL TO ATTAINING A FACILITY FOR SIGHT READING. SECONDLY, THE COMPACT DISC CONTAINS EXERCISE MATERIAL ENABLING YOU TO TEST YOUR OWN UNDERSTANDING OF EACH LESSON. AN INSTRUCTION TO PLAY THE CD IS SHOWN BY THE "PLAY" SYMBOL. THE TWO NUMBERS YOU WILL SEE ALONGSIDE THE SYMBOL INDICATE THE TRACK AND INDEX POINTS YOU NEED TO PROGRAMME ON THE CD PLAYER.

▶ 4 / 7

THE TRACK NUMBER (THE FIRST DIGIT) IS ALWAYS THE SAME AS THE NUMBER OF THE LESSON. INDEX NUMBERS WORK ON MOST CD PLAYERS. THEY ARE LIKE TRACKS WITHIN TRACKS AND CAN USUALLY BE PROGRAMMED IN THE SAME WAY. THE EXAMPLE ABOVE INSTRUCTS YOU TO LISTEN TO THE SEVENTH EXERCISE IN LESSON FOUR.
DON'T WORRY IF YOUR CD PLAYER DOESN'T SHOW INDEX POINTS. THESE TRACKS PLAY THROUGH SEQUENTIALLY ANYWAY, SO YOU CAN JUST AS EASILY USE THE PAUSE BUTTON. IF YOU HAVE A REMOTE CONTROL UNIT FOR YOUR CD PLAYER THIS WILL BE EVEN MORE STRAIGHTFORWARD.

---

is compatible with any style of music, from classical to jazz and rock. It is also is also relevant to every musical instrument. And even if you don't play an instrument, the exercises can be just as easily be performed using the voice alone.

APPROACHING YOUR STUDY

Whatever discipline you hope to attain, the advantage of teaching yourself rather than attending a formal class is that you can work through it at your own pace. A word of warning here, however. As you will quickly discover, the mechanics of learning how to read music are relatively simple, and if, like some people, you have a naturally musical "ear" you will probably find that you can work through this course very quickly. But however well you understand the way written music works, the facility for sight reading – the skill of being able to see a piece of music and immediately sing or play it – will only come with time. And that means one thing – PRACTICE.

A sensible and methodical approach to using the *How To Read Music* course is to set yourself a timetable and try to stick with it. Although working through a single lesson may only take you an hour or so, you should perhaps consider restricting yourself to working through a single lesson each week. In between times, try to get hold of some published sheet music (most reasonable libraries hold at least a small stock) and apply the things you have taught yourself to a "real" example of written music. If possible, take some photocopies so you can mark up the music with a pen. Before you go on to the next lesson, review each previous one – a handy brief summary appears at the end of each lesson – to ensure that you've understood every detail thoroughly.

If you find the task ahead of you a little daunting, here is a final thought. If you spend as little as FIVE MINUTES A DAY reading through ANY piece of written music, marking down the note names and their time values, WITHIN A YEAR you will be able to work through some extremely demanding pieces of music with little difficulty. That's A GUARANTEE.

TERRY BURROWS
LONDON, JUNE 1999

INTRODUCTION:

A Bit of History

We can presume that, no matter how primitive, music has existed for almost as long as man has been able to communicate. However it is only over the past thousand years that well-organized principles allowing music to be written down have existed. Until then, music was passed on orally, just as the great myths and legends had been handed down over the generations.

THE WESTERN TRADITION

Without written music, the musician of the ancient world had two choices when performing. He could either reproduce something that he had already heard or else he had to make it up for himself. Over the past thousand years, the evolution of the Western classical tradition has seen the development of a formalized method by which the most complex compositions can be notated in detail. Indeed, it was the existence of notation that allowed for the development of sophisticated polyphonic music dating from the 17th century onwards. From the point of view of the performer, music when written down could be used as a memory aid and in some cases even obviated the need to have ever heard the music before. Above all, however, notation has helped to preserve the integrity of music itself.

This latter point is especially significant if we compare the way in which music and composition is approached in the West with some of the equally great classical traditions from other cultures of the world. If we consider a piece by classical master such as Mozart, Beethoven or Bach, we take it for granted that their compositions – including the way they notated their own music – is in every way definitive. Thus, we see the principle purpose of notation as being to help the performer reproduce the music as

closely as possible to the original intentions of the composer. We might imagine that if a piano piece by Schumann had been merely passed on orally, within several generations the original would have become somewhat corrupted. And, of course, the notion of a complex orchestral work being passed on orally is quite difficult to imagine.

AROUND THE WORLD

This situation is not necessarily the same in other cultures. In Indian and Oriental music, the role of the performer is less that of an interpreter, and as such alternative means of notation have arisen. Indeed, the Western tonal system that sees an octave divided into twelve equal divisions (the notes A to G on a piano keyboard if you include the black notes) may be inadequate to deal with musical forms that are often completely alien to Western ears.

Some musical cultures use variations on what is known as solmization. This is the naming of each degree of a scale using a phonetic syllable. We all know the song "Do-Re-Mi" from the film The Sound of Music which teaches the European "Sol-fa" system of naming the notes of scale "Do", "Re", "Mi", "Fa", "So", "La", "Ti", "Do". This method has been widely used orally to teach melodies to those who can't read music. Other cultures have developed their own equivalents over the ages, such as the Indian "Sa", "Ri", "Ga", Ma", "Pa", "Dha", "Ni" or "Kung", "Shang", "Chiao", "Chih", "Yü" in China or "Ding", "Dong", "Deng", "Dung", "Dang" in Bali.

THE NEW STANDARD

The musical notation we have come to use in the West is immediately recognizable to us all, even if we can't actually understand its meaning. Circles with different characteristics to represent how long a note should be sounded are arranged on a five-line staff from which the pitch of the note can be deduced. A variety of graphic symbols can be marked alongside the music to further instruct the performer the volume at which notes should be played. This covers the three basic characteristics of any single note: pitch, duration and volume. However, the evolution that has brought us to this point has taken thousands of years.

THE MODERN ORAL TRADITION

∞∞∞∞

THE VAST MAJORITY OF FOLK AND POPULAR MUSIC CONTINUES TO BE LEARNED AND PASSED ON ORALLY. HOWEVER THIS PROCESS HAS BEEN RADICALLY CHANGED BY THE DEVELOPMENT OF RECORDING TECHNOLOGY SINCE THE START OF THE TWENTIETH CENTURY. THIS CAPABILITY THAT ALLOWS THE MUSICIAN TO LISTEN REPEATEDLY TO A RECORDING OR BROADCAST HAS PROVIDED AN ALTERNATIVE WAY OF LEARNING AND PASSING ON POPULAR SONGS WITHOUT HAVING TO READ MUSIC. IT ALSO CONTINUES TO ACT AS A MEANS OF PRESERVING THE DEFINITIVE VERSIONS OF ORIGINAL WORKS.

THE EVOLUTION OF MUSICAL NOTATION

Although there would seem to be evidence that some form of written music existed in Ancient Egypt as long ago as 3000 BC, the basis from which modern Western musical notation evolved can truly be said to have begun in Ancient Greece. It was here that the system of naming different pitches with letters was first adopted. Unfortunately, although there are a number of existing written fragments, they have left us with very few clues as to how the music of that period might have sounded. One thing we can be sure of, however, is the importance of the great philosophers of Ancient Greece on the development of Western musical theory.

The most influential of the early theoreticians were the Pythagoreans, for whom music and mathematics were inextricably linked. Pythagorus, who lived around 550 BC, was himself said to have calculated the way in which pitch changed when the length of a vibrating string was altered, his followers eventually noting the mathematical ratios that were needed to create the most pleasing intervals. They found that halving the length of the string created the octave – the same note but in a higher register. Similarly that a ratios of 4:3 and 3:2 produced the most pleasing intervals (known to the modern musician as the "perfect fourth" and "perfect fifth" respectively), in effect, defining consonant sound.

Two hundred years later, the influence of Plato and Aristotle could be seen on the most important of the Ancient Greek music theorists, Aristoxenus. A former pupil of Aristotle, Aristoxenus wrote the earliest known treatise on musical theory. Among his ideas was the view that pitch was a long line within which an infinite number of subdivisions could exist. This later allowed for the naming of specific pitches with letters taken from the Ionian alphabet. Some of the terminology used at this time would re-emerge in Europe almost a thousand years later where, via the influence of the church, the work of Aristotle and Plato would help shape the very basis of modern Western thinking.

NEUMIC NOTATION

Unsurprisingly, perhaps, it was the music of the early European church that oversaw the birth of a form of notation that would slowly evolve into that which we use today. Arising form the Christian plainchant of the ninth century, a system which we now know as NEUMIC NOTATION came into use. At first it was little more than a set of a instructions for singers who were already familiar with the melody and words: these "simple neumes" were used to represent pitch directions (up or down) and vocal ornamentation. By around the year 1100, the system had developed so that the neumes were laid out so as to suggest melody lines. Pitches were fixed by marking the neumes on four horizontal lines of music, representing the pitch of the note. For the first time, this enabled a singer to perform an unfamiliar melody.

Along with the recognition of different vocal ranges came a need for a way of notating a wider range of notes. At first, colours were used to give the lines of music a context, for example, one line being drawn in red to signify the note C (and thus defining the notes on the other staves). Eventually, the letter of the key note was positioned at the start of the staff. The notes F, G and C were used for this purpose, to provide different note ranges for different registers. These letters were gradually stylized and eventually

evolved into the clef symbols that are still found in music today.

G	F	C
(TREBLE)	(BASS)	(C CLEF)

FRANCO OF COLOGNE

By the year 1200, neumic notation had began to take on some of the characteristics of the modern system, including the addition of the fifth staff line. Around 1260, time values were first applied to notes when a system we now know as MENSURAL NOTATION was codified by Franco of Cologne. It was he, influenced by Aristoxenus, who devised a system of notes made up of proportional subdivisions. The note values were known by the names *maxima*, *long*, *breve*, *semibreve* and *minim* – the latter three terms remain in use today. These symbols appeared on the staff as filled squares or diamond-shapes with stems.

To accommodate a variety of rhythmic effects, Franco also made it possible to split the named notes into subdivisions of either two or three. These were termed "imperfect" (a division of two) and "perfect" (a division of three). Combining these different note values made it possible to produce a wider variety of rhythmic effects.

By around 1400, further subdivisions were added to allow the notation of music of greater subtlety – the *fusa* (sometimes called the semi-minim) and the *semifusa*. These were indicated with one or two "flags" on top of the stems.

THE MODERN SYSTEM

The mensural system was used until around 1600, after which it gradually evolved into the earliest form of the notation we now recognize. During this time, the notes themselves became rounded and were grouped together according to their values. However, the most significant change was the abandonment of the idea of perfect and imperfect notes in favour of one that simply used the two-to-one relationship. From that point onward, whenever a note was required to be split into three, it was simply indicated followed by a dot.

This period also saw a substantial change in music theory. Music written for plainsong, such as Gregorian chanting, had invariably been composed using notes drawn from a series of sequences known as MODES. Each mode was a scale made up from a fixed set of pitch intervals, and thus each had its own unique character. The eight modes used were Dorian, Hypodorian, Phrygian, Hypophrygian, Lydian, Hypolydian, Mixolydian, and Hypomixolydian. By the middle ages, notated melodies were listed according to their mode in liturgical books or tonaries.

The Renaissance saw a change in compositional practice which led to the creation of four new modes, two of which were known as Aeolian and Ionian. By the seventeenth century, the use of these two new modes became widespread and they soon evolved into the major and minor scale systems that have

dominated Western music ever since then. The principle difference was that whilst the modes were made up of fixed notes, the major and minor systems took the intervals of tones and semitones from the Aeolian and Ionian modes and applied them so that they could begin on every note.

TO THE PRESENT DAY

The development of written music since this time has been one of refinement, the main additions being the emergence of a multitude of shorthand terms that indicate the way a piece of music should be played. These can vary from changes in tempo to dynamic elements such as volume.

As music has developed, the inherently limiting nature of traditional music notation has sometimes shown its inflexibility. In some cases, composers of contemporary classical music have found it easier to develop entirely new approaches geared to their own music. However, the traditional system continues to evolve and remains the most universally accepted approach, especially in the classical realm.

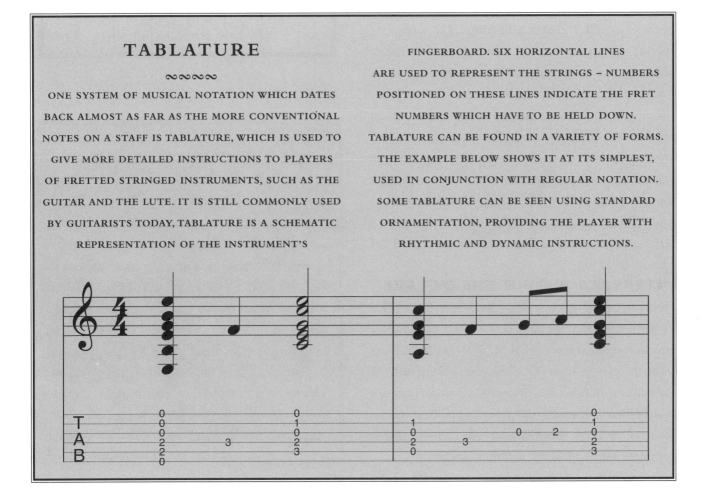

TABLATURE

∞∾∾∾

ONE SYSTEM OF MUSICAL NOTATION WHICH DATES BACK ALMOST AS FAR AS THE MORE CONVENTIONAL NOTES ON A STAFF IS TABLATURE, WHICH IS USED TO GIVE MORE DETAILED INSTRUCTIONS TO PLAYERS OF FRETTED STRINGED INSTRUMENTS, SUCH AS THE GUITAR AND THE LUTE. IT IS STILL COMMONLY USED BY GUITARISTS TODAY, TABLATURE IS A SCHEMATIC REPRESENTATION OF THE INSTRUMENT'S FINGERBOARD. SIX HORIZONTAL LINES ARE USED TO REPRESENT THE STRINGS – NUMBERS POSITIONED ON THESE LINES INDICATE THE FRET NUMBERS WHICH HAVE TO BE HELD DOWN. TABLATURE CAN BE FOUND IN A VARIETY OF FORMS. THE EXAMPLE BELOW SHOWS IT AT ITS SIMPLEST, USED IN CONJUNCTION WITH REGULAR NOTATION. SOME TABLATURE CAN BE SEEN USING STANDARD ORNAMENTATION, PROVIDING THE PLAYER WITH RHYTHMIC AND DYNAMIC INSTRUCTIONS.

LESSON 1:

Introducing Pitch

Think of a simple song that almost everyone knows, for example "When The Saints Go Marching In". If you sing the first line of the tune – "Oh, when the saints…" – you will notice that it's made up from four completely different notes. As you sing through the phrase, the sound of each note rises higher than the last one. This variation is called PITCH.

HIGH AND LOW NOTES

If you play "When the Saints Go Marching In" on a piano keyboard, you will find that each successive note would be to right of the previous one. Playing notes to the right makes the pitch is HIGHER; the opposite direction makes it LOWER. On a stringed instrument, by moving the hand along the finger-board towards the bridge the pitch increases; moving towards the tuning pegs causes the pitch to decrease.

Every note you hear sung or played on a musical instrument has its own pitch. Each key on the piano also has its own pitch. The pitch of a note can be defined scientifically in terms of the frequency of its sound waves. Similarly, in music, a pitch is a fixed sound which can be identified using a series of letters ranging from A to G.   ▶ 1 / 1

INTERVALS WITHIN THE OCTAVE

Doubling the frequency of a note increases its pitch by an octave. Within that octave, there are twelve equal divisions, known as SEMITONES. By playing through each of these divisions you will move from the starting note to the octave in 12 steps. This can best be heard in relation to a piano keyboard. Listen to track 1/2 of the CD and you will hear the complete range of notes within a single octave starting from the note A.   ▶ 1 / 2

OH, WHEN THE SAINTS…

HEARING OCTAVES
∞∞∞

HERE IS AN EXPERIMENT FOR YOU TO TRY OUT. START TO HUM A NOTE, HOLDING THE PITCH STEADY FOR A FEW SECONDS. NOW GRADUALLY INCREASE THE PITCH WHILE YOU ARE HUMMING. AT ONE POINT – AND YOU'LL KNOW IMMEDIATELY WHEN THIS HAPPENS – YOU WILL HIT A NOTE WHICH NATURALLY SOUNDS VERY SIMILAR TO THE ONE YOU STARTED WITH. EVEN THOUGH THIS NEW NOTE IS CLEARLY HIGHER IN PITCH THAN THE ORIGINAL, BOTH OF THEM WOULD BE GIVEN THE SAME NAME. THESE TWO NOTES WHICH YOU HAVE JUST SUNG ARE SEPARATED IN PITCH BY A FIXED INTERVAL CALLED AN OCTAVE.

TEST 1

THIS FIRST EXERCISE IS A SIMPLE SET OF PITCH TESTS. ON THE NEXT EIGHT TRACKS ON THE CD, YOU WILL HEAR EIGHT SETS OF FOUR-NOTE SEQUENCES. THREE OF THE NOTES IN EACH SET HAVE THE SAME PITCH, BUT ONE IS DIFFER-ENT. YOUR TASK IS TO IDENTIFY THE ODD ONE OUT IN EACH GROUP – A, B, C OR D. YOU CAN FIND THE ANSWERS ON PAGE 120.

1. ▶ 1 / 3   2. ▶ 1 / 4
3. ▶ 1 / 5   4. ▶ 1 / 6
5. ▶ 1 / 7   6. ▶ 1 / 8
7. ▶ 1 / 9   8. ▶ 1 / 10

NAMING THE NOTES

All of the white notes on a standard piano keyboard have names within the range of letters between A and G (don't worry about the black notes for the time being). These same seven notes can be represented in written music using a grid of five horizontal lines known as a STAFF or STAVE (but always STAVES in the plural). A variety of symbols are placed on or between the lines to indicate the pitch of a note and how long it lasts.

However, as you can see from the example below, this only allows for a range of nine different pitches. You only have to look at a piano keyboard to see that there are a good many more than that. This problem is overcome by positioning what is known as a CLEF symbol at the front of the staff. There are a number of different types of clef, although the most common is the treble clef. It is also known as a G CLEF, because the centre of the figure always starts on the second line from the bottom. This defines that line as representing the note G. This, in turn, means that we can work out all the other notes on the treble clef from that point.

The diagram below shows a limited range of notes on a piano keyboard and how they are represented on the treble staff.   ▶ 1 / 11

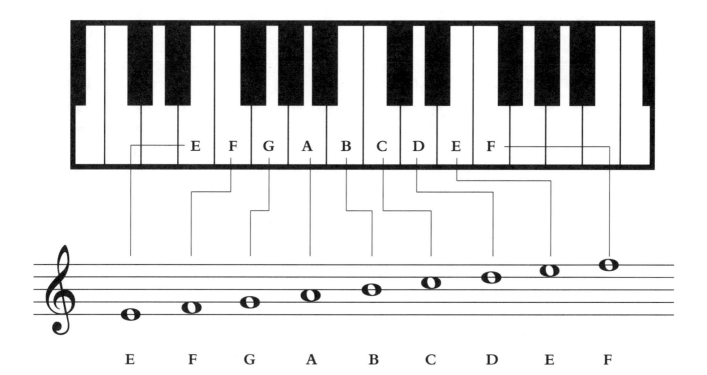

LEDGER LINES

The problem with the staff as it is presented on the previous page is that it can only represent a range of nine pitches – from E on the bottom line to F on the top line. This range can be extended by using what are known as ledger lines. Quite simply, where a note goes off the edge of the staff, additional lines can be added for that note only. The two staves below show how the staff can be extended to cover a range of more than two octaves.

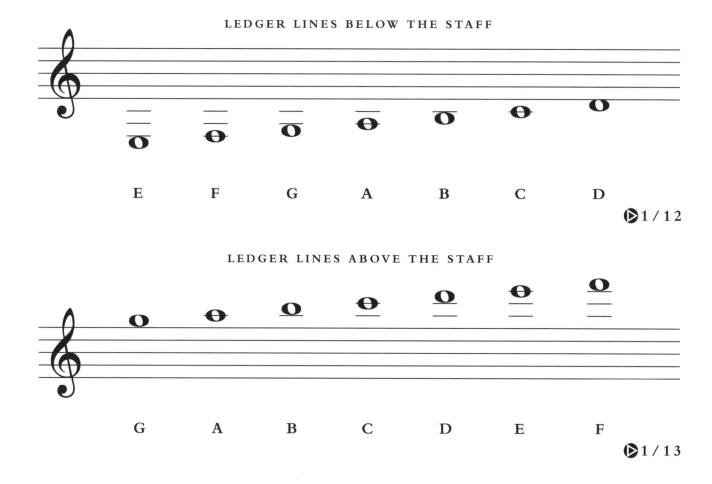

LEDGER LINES BELOW THE STAFF

E   F   G   A   B   C   D

▶ 1 / 12

LEDGER LINES ABOVE THE STAFF

G   A   B   C   D   E   F

▶ 1 / 13

NAMING THE LINES AND SPACES

When referring to the lines or spaces that make up the staff, they are always named from the bottom upwards. hence the bottom line is known as the first line and the top line the fifth line. Similarly the space between the first and second lines is known as the first space. In all there are five lines and four spaces.

Learning to name the lines and spaces is the most fundamental lesson of being able to sight read. Over the ages many different approaches have been taken to get novices to the point where they can identify a note automatically. One of the most popular methods for beginners has been to devise mnemonic phrases as memory aids. The notes on the line of treble staff are E-G-B-D-F. These can be learned by remembering the phrase "EVERY GOOD BOY DESERVES FAVOURS", or sometimes "EAT GOOD BREAD DEAR FATHER" Indeed, you'll find that every music teachers has his or her own preferred memory jogger. The notes on the spaces are much easier to remember as they spell out the word "FACE".

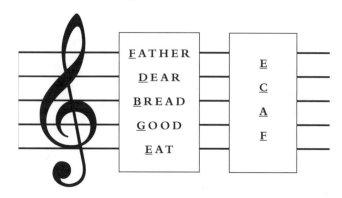

TEST 2

〰〰〰〰

HERE ARE FIVE STAVES OF MUSIC, EACH ONE SHOWING EIGHT DIFFERENTLY PITCHED NOTES. YOUR TASK IS SIMPLY TO NAME EACH NOTE ON EACH STAFF. TO MAKE THINGS MORE OF A CHALLENGE FOR YOU, SOME OF THE NOTES HAVE BEEN POSITIONED ON OR BETWEEN LEDGER LINES, AND THUS STAND OUTSIDE OF THE BASIC STAFF. IT'S WORTH TRYING OUT THE MNEMONIC PHRASES TO HELP YOU REMEMBER THE NAMES OF THE NOTES. ON A TREBLE STAFF THEY ARE "EAT GOOD BREAD DEAR FATHER" FOR NOTES ON THE LINES, AND "FACE" FOR THOSE ON THE SPACES. WHEN YOU'VE COMPLETED THE TEST, YOU CAN CHECK YOUR ANSWERS ON PAGE 120.

EXERCISE 1.

EXERCISE 2.

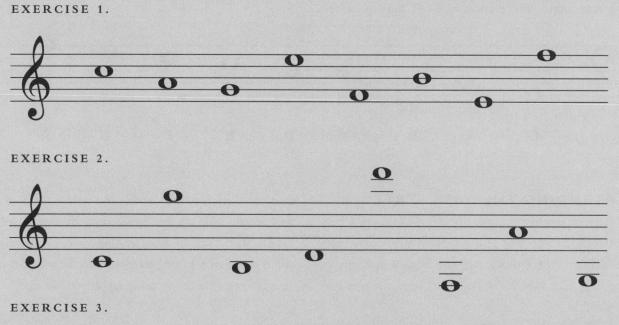

EXERCISE 3.

EXERCISE 4.

EXERCISE 5.

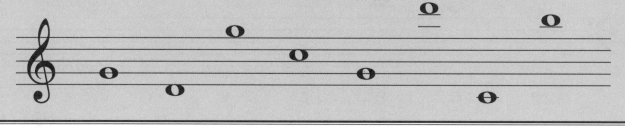

THE BASS CLEF

So far, we have seen a range of just over three octaves – E on the lowest ledger line to G on the highest ledger line. But that's a range of just 39 notes (if you include the black notes): a standard modern grand piano has a range of over seven octaves, so, how are these extra notes shown in written music? The answer is to use a different kind of clef – the BASS CLEF.

By replacing the treble clef with a bass clef, the notes on the lines and spaces of that staff take on different names and pitches. You can remember the notes on lines of the bass clef using the phrase "GOOD BOYS DESERVE FUN ALWAYS", and the spaces with "A COW EATS GRASS".

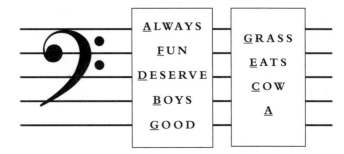

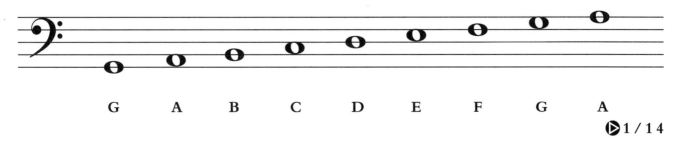

G   A   B   C   D   E   F   G   A

▶ 1 / 14

EXTENDING THE BASS STAFF

Ledger lines can be used to extend notes on a bass staff in the same way as the treble staff. In this case, they move from F downward and from B upwards. In the examples shown for both clefs only three ledger lines have been named above and below the staff. In fact ledger lines can be notated to create far wider ranges than this. In practice, however, the music is often easier to read if these notes are shown on a staff in a different range, by using an alternative clef.

LEDGER LINES BELOW THE STAFF

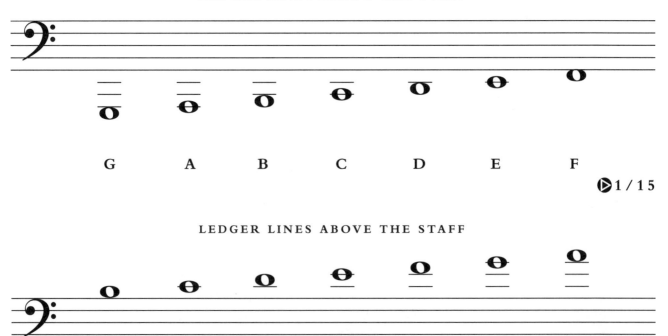

G   A   B   C   D   E   F

▶ 1 / 15

LEDGER LINES ABOVE THE STAFF

B   C   D   E   F   G   A

▶ 1 / 16

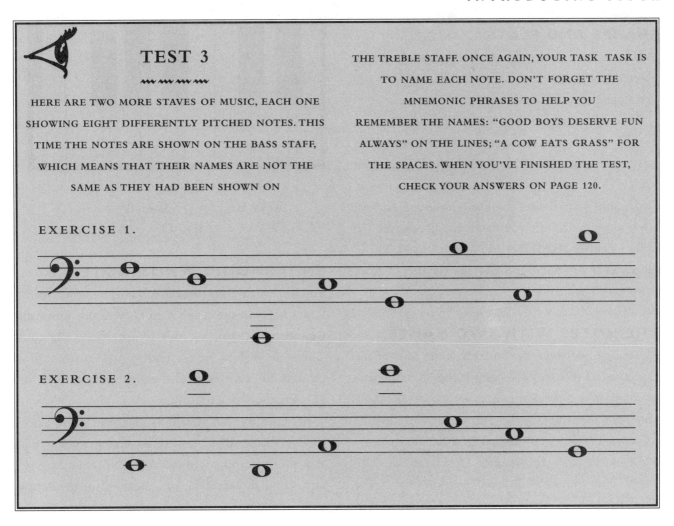

TEST 3

HERE ARE TWO MORE STAVES OF MUSIC, EACH ONE SHOWING EIGHT DIFFERENTLY PITCHED NOTES. THIS TIME THE NOTES ARE SHOWN ON THE BASS STAFF, WHICH MEANS THAT THEIR NAMES ARE NOT THE SAME AS THEY HAD BEEN SHOWN ON THE TREBLE STAFF. ONCE AGAIN, YOUR TASK TASK IS TO NAME EACH NOTE. DON'T FORGET THE MNEMONIC PHRASES TO HELP YOU REMEMBER THE NAMES: "GOOD BOYS DESERVE FUN ALWAYS" ON THE LINES; "A COW EATS GRASS" FOR THE SPACES. WHEN YOU'VE FINISHED THE TEST, CHECK YOUR ANSWERS ON PAGE 120.

EXERCISE 1.

EXERCISE 2.

THE COMPLETE RANGE

Because it has a wider range of notes than most other musical instruments, music composed specifically for the piano is nearly always written over two staves that are shown concurrently. The curly bracket shown at the beginning indicates that the two staves are to be played simultaneously. As a general rule, the pianist's left hand plays the notes on the bass staff, and the right hand plays the notes on the treble staff, although this is by no means always the case.

The example below shows a range of nine notes played over both staves. You will notice that there is a crossover point where the notes could be written on either staff. This separation is usually governed by the musical context. The note C in this register is referred to as MIDDLE C.   ▶1 / 17

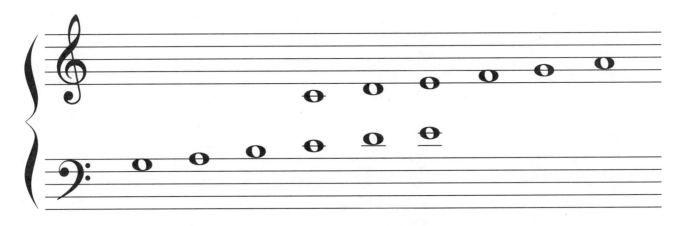

G   A   B   C   D   E   F   G   A

SHARPS AND FLATS

So far we have concentrated naming the the white notes of the piano keyboard. Now it's time to turn our attention to the black notes.

Since the white notes have already been allocated a sequence of letters between A and G, it seems fairly reasonable that the black notes should take their names from the white notes they sit between. Depending on whether the black note is higher or lower in pitch than the white note it will be given the suffix of either SHARP or FLAT respectively. This is shown in music notation using the symbols "♯" for a sharp and "♭" for a flat.

THE NOTES WITH TWO NAMES

As you can see from the diagram at the foot of the page, the fact that they take their names from the surrounding white notes means that each of the black notes can have one of two names. It can either be named as a "sharpened" equivalent to the note immediately to its left – for example F♯ (referred to as "F sharp") – or else as a "flattened" version of the note immediately to its right – for example B♭ (referred to as "B flat"). Notes such as these are said to be ENHARMONIC. As you will see later in the course, although it may seem logical, these names are not interchangeable. To be totally accurate, the name used is wholly dependent on the musical context, but you needn't worry about this for the moment – it will become clearer as you progress.

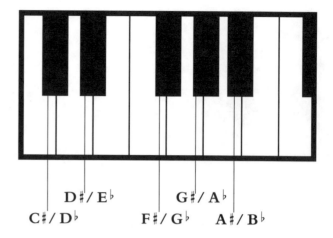

ENHARMONIC WHITE NOTES?

You might have imagined that the names given to the white notes in the range A to G were unequivocally unambiguous. And yet this is not always the case. There are, in fact, some circumstances in which it is possible for various of the white notes to take on enharmonic characteristics.

In some musical situations you may come across the note names B♯, C♭, and E♯, all of which if you look at a piano keyboard would seem NOT to exist. In fact, although occurring in a technical or theoretical sense, sometimes it may be necessary to follow a set of harmonic rules that require you to sharpen or flatten certain notes. If, for example, you flatten the note C – that is you reduce its pitch by a semitone – it becomes C♭, even though the pitch is identical to the note B. Similarly, the notes B♯ and E♯ are all valid possible names, even though they are identical in pitch to the notes C and F respectively.

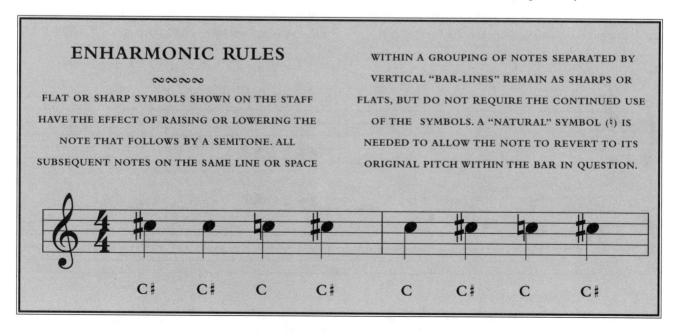

ENHARMONIC RULES

∽∽∽∽

FLAT OR SHARP SYMBOLS SHOWN ON THE STAFF HAVE THE EFFECT OF RAISING OR LOWERING THE NOTE THAT FOLLOWS BY A SEMITONE. ALL SUBSEQUENT NOTES ON THE SAME LINE OR SPACE WITHIN A GROUPING OF NOTES SEPARATED BY VERTICAL "BAR-LINES" REMAIN AS SHARPS OR FLATS, BUT DO NOT REQUIRE THE CONTINUED USE OF THE SYMBOLS. A "NATURAL" SYMBOL (♮) IS NEEDED TO ALLOW THE NOTE TO REVERT TO ITS ORIGINAL PITCH WITHIN THE BAR IN QUESTION.

ENHARMONIC EQUIVALENTS

In the list below, all eight enharmonic possibilities are shown alongside their alternative note names. In each example you will notice that no two enharmonic equivalents occupy the same line or space on the staff.

The theory behind which of the two note names is appropriate to use will become clearer when you have acquired a greater understanding of the way in which scales, intervals and chords work. These are covered in lessons 3 and beyond.

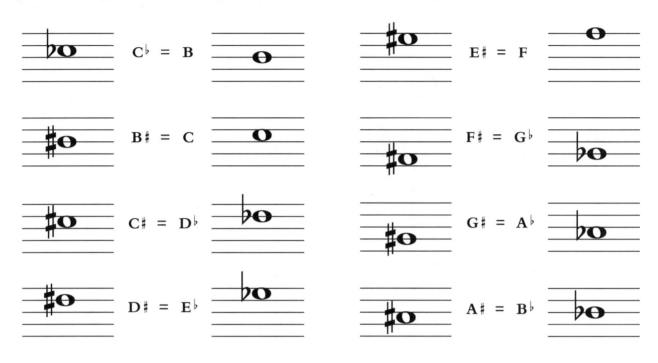

C♭ = B   B♯ = C   C♯ = D♭   D♯ = E♭   E♯ = F   F♯ = G♭   G♯ = A♭   A♯ = B♭

TONE AND SEMITONE INTERVALS

The enharmonic notes have been added to the two staves below. The top staff treats all the enharmonic notes as sharps and the bottom staff treats them as flats. In both cases the pitch of the notes (and hence the entire sequence) will sound identical.

The distance in pitch between each of the notes is a semitone. In most Western music this is the smallest pitch interval, although some twentieth-century composers have experimented with smaller divisions known as microtones. An interval of two semitones – for example between the notes F and G – is referred to as a TONE. Listen to the difference between the two sequences on track 1/18 of the CD. The first plays the 13 semitone intervals between C and C within an octave. The second plays just the eight white notes which is made up of intervals of tones and semitones.   ▶ 1 / 18

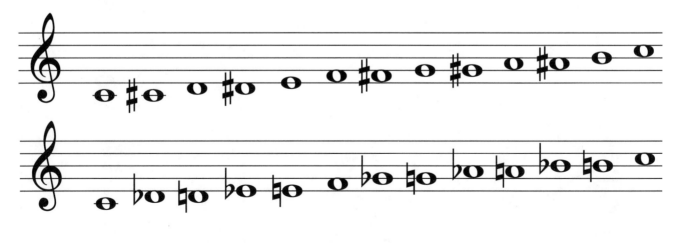

C   C♯/D♭   D   D♯/E♭   E   F   F♯/G♭   G   G♯/A♭   A   A♯/B♭   B   C

TEST 4

〜〜〜〜〜

TAKE A LOOK AT THE FIVE STAVES OF MUSIC SHOWN BELOW. EACH ONE CONTAINS EIGHT DIFFERENTLY PITCHED NOTES, MOST OF WHICH ARE SHOWN EITHER AS A SHARP OR FLAT. YOUR TASK IS TO IDENTIFY THE CORRECT NOTE NAMES.

PAY SPECIAL ATTENTION TO THE "NATURAL" SYMBOLS – IT'S QUITE EASY TO GET THEM MIXED UP WITH THE SHARP SIGNS. REMEMBER THAT THE EFFECT OF THE NATURAL SYMBOL IS TO RETURN THE "SHARPENED" OR "FLATTENED" NOTE TO IT'S ORIGINAL PITCH – A SEMITONE HIGHER OR LOWER. THE ANSWERS ARE ON PAGE 120.

EXERCISE 1.

EXERCISE 2.

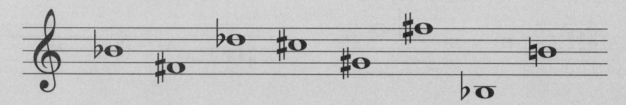

EXERCISE 3.

EXERCISE 4.

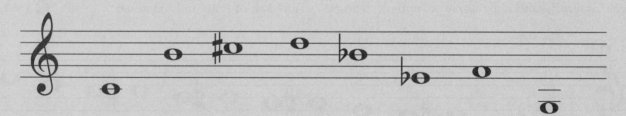

EXERCISE 5.

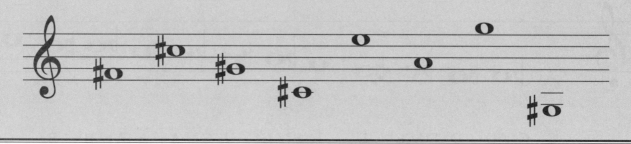

TEST 5

~~~ ~~~ ~~~ ~~~

THIS IS A VERY DEMANDING LISTENING TEST, SO YOU SHOULD REVIEW THIS ONE SEVERAL TIMES BEFORE YOU DECIDE ON YOUR ANSWERS. EACH OF THE STAVES BELOW HAS AN EQUIVALENT TRACK ON THE CD. IN EACH CASE, THREE OF THE FOUR NOTES ARE CORRECT – ONE OF THEM IS WRONG. YOUR TASK IS TO IDENTIFY WHICH IS THE ODD NOTE OUT.

IT'S A GOOD IDEA TO BEGIN EACH EXERCISE BY WORKING OUT THE NOTES NAMES AND THEN SINGING OR PLAYING THEM FOR YOURSELF UNTIL YOU ARE FAMILIAR WITH THE PATTERN OR TUNE. YOU CAN THEN LISTEN TO THE RELEVANT TRACK ON THE CD. NOTE THAT IF YOU ARE SINGING THE EXERCISES AND DON'T HAVE A PITCH REFERENCE, YOU CAN USE THE FIRST NOTE OF THE SEQUENCE TO GET YOUR BEARINGS. YOU CAN CHECK THE ANSWERS ON PAGE 120.

EXERCISE 1. ▶ 1 / 19

EXERCISE 2. ▶ 1 / 20

EXERCISE 3. ▶ 1 / 21

EXERCISE 4. ▶ 1 / 22

EXERCISE 5. ▶ 1 / 23

EXERCISE 6. ▶ 1 / 24

TIME OUT: SUMMARY OF LESSON 1

∾∾∾∾

HERE IS A SUMMARY OF THE MAIN POINTS OF THIS LESSON. IF YOU HAVE ANY DOUBTS ABOUT ANYTHING LISTED BELOW YOU SHOULD REVIEW IT BEFORE GOING ON TO LESSON 2.

- MEANING OF PITCH
- MEANING OF OCTAVE
- UNDERSTANDING OF THE STAFF
- UNDERSTANDING OF LEDGER LINES
- NAMING THE NOTES ON A TREBLE CLEF

- NAMING THE NOTES ON THE BASS CLEF
- UNDERSTANDING FLATS AND SHARPS
- UNDERSTANDING ENHARMONIC EQUIVALENTS
- UNDERSTANDING THE "NATURAL SYMBOL"
- DIFFERENCE BETWEEN TONES AND SEMITONE

LESSON 2:

Timing and Rhythm

You are now able to identify the names of notes written on a staff, even if it takes a while before this becomes second nature. However, while this tells you the pitch of the note that needs to be played or sung, what it fails to indicate is WHEN the note should be played, and HOW LONG it should be sustained. For this you must be able to interpret note values.

HEARING THE BEAT

If you listen to any piece of music you will hear a pulsing effect. This is the RHYTHM of music. If you now clap along to the music, you are almost certain to find yourself naturally drawn to a consistent beat. Irrespective of the TEMPO of the music – how fast it is being played, that is – the time interval between each clap will be the same value as all of the others.

The most common type of beat you will hear groups together four CROTCHETS. You will find that that you can count along to most types of music by repeating the numbers one to four. In doing so, you will usually find that music naturally emphasises the first beat. This natural grouping of beats is known in written music as a BAR.

The same principle applies to the time values of notes sung or played by a musical instrument. A CROTCHET is shown in written music as a filled circle with a "stem". Depending on the position of the note on the staff, the stem can point in either direction. The convention is that notes on and above

the third line have downward-pointing stems; below that the stems point upwards.

CROTCHET

The piece of music shown at the foot of the page is made up of two bars. The two numbers that follow the treble clef at the beginning of the staff together make up what is known as the TIME SIGNATURE. The number four written above another four denotes that the piece is in FOUR-FOUR time, and that there are four beats in the bar. This time signature is by far the most widely used – so much so, in fact, that it is also known as COMMON TIME. Listen to track 2/1 of the CD – the notes can be heard alongside a rhythmic click.

The way in which the lower number works will be explained in more depth during lesson 4.

NOTE VALUES

All of the examples you have seen written down so far have featured notes of the same value or duration. If you sing any familiar tune, it will be immediately clear that some of the notes are sustained longer than others. Like many elements of music, the way in which note durations are shown in notation works along basic mathematical principles – indeed, the philosopher Gottfried Wilhelm Leibniz (1646-1716) described music as "unconscious arithmetic".

MULTIPLES AND DIVISIONS

The value of any note is fixed to its relationship to the semibreve. The semibreve can be subdivided four times by the crotchet – the note value which forms the beat in the vast majority of western music. One way or another, all notes can be viewed as being either multiples or a divisions of a crotchet. This is an important point to grasp in understanding written music. The descriptions of the sub-divisions that follow all assume a time signature of four-four – hence each beat is crotchet.

SEMIBREVES

The longest note value usually found in modern music is a SEMIBREVE, which sustains over four beats. This means that it lasts for the same amount of time it takes to play four crotchets. As its name suggests, there is such a term as a BREVE, which is twice the length of a semibreve, however, this is a somewhat archaic note value which has found little use in the twentieth century. A semibreve is shown in written music as a hollow circle – it has no stem.

𝐨

SEMIBREVE

The first staff below contains a single semibreve. If you listen to track 2/2 on the CD you will hear how the note sustains over four beats, audible as clicks. Count along with the clicks as shown under the staff.

MINIM

A note that sustains over two beats is called a MINIM. This appears in written music as a hollow circle with a stem.

MINIM

The staff shown at the foot of the page contains a pair of minims. If you play track 2/3 of the CD you will hear that each minim sustains over two beats. Again, four bars of this example can be heard on the CD.

SEMIBREVE BAR (FOUR BEATS)

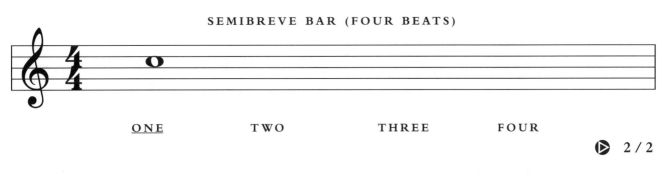

ONE   TWO   THREE   FOUR

▶ 2 / 2

MINIM BAR (TWO BEATS)

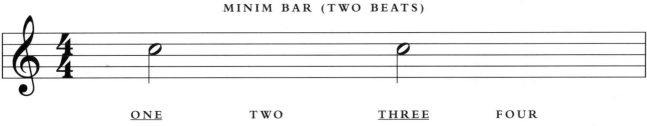

ONE   TWO   THREE   FOUR

▶ 2 / 3

QUAVERS AND BEYOND

Notes with a time value less than a crotchet are called QUAVERS, of which there are a number of different levels of subdivision. The first such subdivision is a SEMIQUAVER – subsequent divisions are DEMI-SEMIQUAVERS and, on rare occasions, HEMI-DEMISEMIQUAVERS.

Once again, the descriptions that follow all assume a time signature of four-four so that each beat has the value of a crotchet.

QUAVER

A quaver is half the value of a crotchet – in a bar with a time signature of four-four it lasts for half a beat. It is written on the staff as a crotchet with a FLAG (sometimes also called a TAIL).

QUAVER

THE COMPONENTS OF
A NOTE

∾∾∾∾

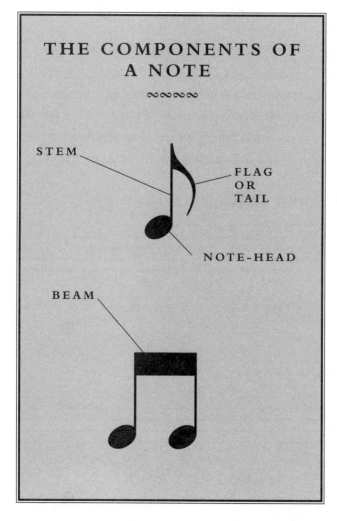

STEM

FLAG
OR
TAIL

NOTE-HEAD

BEAM

To make music easier to read, groups of two or four quavers can be joined together with a BEAM.

A beam is a line that joins the tips of two or more stems. It can be applied which ever direction the stem is pointing.

SEMIQUAVERS

A note which is a quarter of the value of a crotchet is called a semiquaver. It can be identified from the "double flag" on its stem.

SEMIQUAVER

Like the quaver examples shown above, grouped semiquavers can also be joined together by beam. A semiquaver beam consists of two horizontal lines joing the tip of the stem.

FURTHER DIVISIONS

A semiquaver can be halved again to produce a demisemiquaver – an eighth of a crotchet. In relatively rare cases, a further subdivision to a sixteenth of a crotchet is also possible - this is known as a hemidemisemiquaver.

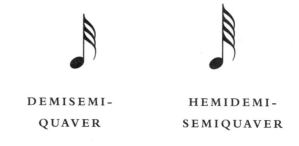

DEMISEMI-
QUAVER

HEMIDEMI-
SEMIQUAVER

COUNTING QUAVER DIVISIONS

Each of the four staves shown below contain a single bar of notes. The first staff contains four crotchets, each of which has a duration of a single beat. This is shown merely for comparison to the subsequent staves – you should already be familiar with idea of counting four beats in the bar.

The second example contains eight quavers - or half beats. A common way to count quavers is by inserting the word "and" between each of the beats. If you take a listen to tracks 2/4 and 2/5 on the CD, you will hear that the tempo of the beats on the two staves is identical, but in the latter example there are four additional note sounds inserted in the spaces between each beat.

SEMIQUAVERS AND BEYOND

Divisions below the quaver can be difficult to follow. At a slow tempo it is possible to split the syllables, so that you count out <u>ONE</u>-UN-AN-AND-<u>TWO</u>-OO-AN-AND-<u>THREE</u>-EE-AN-AND-<u>FOUR</u>-OR-AN-AND. At a faster tempo, or where demisemiquavers are involved, you will not be able to count that quickly. The alternative is to multiply the numbering, splitting a bar of four-four into a count of eight or even sixteen.

CROTCHET BAR (ONE BEAT)

ONE   TWO   THREE   FOUR

▶ 2 / 4

QUAVER BAR (HALF BEATS)

ONE   AND   TWO   AND   THREE   AND   FOUR   AND

▶ 2 / 5

SEMIQUAVER BAR (QUARTER BEATS)

ONE   AND   TWO   AND   THREE   AND   FOUR   AND

▶ 2 / 6

DEMISEMIQUAVER BAR (EIGHTH BEATS)

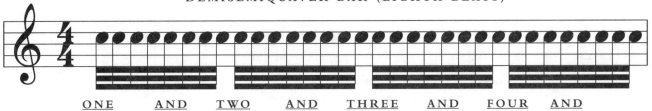

ONE   AND   TWO   AND   THREE   AND   FOUR   AND

▶ 2 / 7

MIXING NOTE VALUES

As we have already seen, within any written piece of music, the notes are grouped in bars according to the time signature – the numbers at the beginning of the staff. All the pieces so far seen have been in four-four time, which means that the value of the notes in a bar adds up to four beats: a bar of four crotchets is "worth" four beats, as is a bar of eight quavers, sixteen semiquavers, two minims or one semibreve. All music, regardless of its style, takes its natural rhythm from the way in which the notes are grouped or accented within a bar. To achieve this effect, notes of different time values need to be combined within the same bar.

Try out the following example. Look at the two staves shown below. First count out the note values on every beat as shown beneath each note. Remember that a crotchet lasts for one beat, a minim for two beats and a semibreve for four beats. After you've

managed that, tap or clap out the rhythm according to the note values. This means ONLY tapping on the first beat of the note. Thus the sequence will be TAP-TAP-TAP-SILENCE-TAP-TAP-TAP-SILENCE-TAP-TAP-TAP-TAP-TAP-SILENCE-SILENCE-SILENCE. (In practice, of course, each beat of silence represents the previous note being sustained – this exercise merely illustrates how the rhythm is created.) Now put the two together, tapping out the rhythm and counting out the beat values at the same time.

Notice how, irrespective of the individual notes, the combined time value of the bar is always four. The first two bars each contain two crotchets and a minim (1+1+2 beats = 4 beats). The third bar has four crotchets (1+1+1+1 beats = 4 beats). The fourth bar contains one semibreve (4 beats = 4 beats). This rule ALWAYS applies to any piece of music written in four-four time.   ▶ 2 / 8

MIXING IN QUAVERS

Here is an example that makes use of quavers. These are harder to count, because their value is half a beat, so you must count out two quavers for every single

beat. Take the same approach to this example as you did above, first counting out the beats as shown below the staff, and then tapping out the rhythm of the note values.   ▶ 2 / 9

TEST 6

∿∿ ∿∿ ∿∿ ∿∿

CONTINUING THE THEME OF UNDERSTANDING THE WAY NOTE VALUES ARE USED TO CREATE RHYTHMS, HERE ARE A FURTHER FIVE TWO-BAR EXERCISES FOR YOU TO WORK THROUGH. IN EACH CASE YOU MUST NAME THE NOTE VALUE AND BE ABLE TO CORRECTLY TAP OUT THE RHYTHM. AS IN THE PREVIOUS EXERCISES, WE ARE NOT CONCERNED WITH THE PITCH OF THE NOTE AT THE MOMENT BUT SIMPLY ITS TIME VALUE. WATCH OUT FOR EXERCISE FIVE, WHICH CONTAINS SEMIQUAVERS. REMEMBER, A CROTCHET IS THE EQUIVALENT TO EIGHT SEMIQUAVERS AND SO NEEDS TO BE COUNTED OUT ACCORDINGLY. YOU CAN HEAR THE ANSWERS ON THE CD.

EXERCISE 1. ▷ 2/10

EXERCISE 2. ▷ 2/11

EXERCISE 3. ▷ 2/12

EXERCISE 4. ▷ 2/13

EXERCISE 5. ▷ 2/14

ADDITIONAL NOTE VALUES

You can think of the basic note values outlined on the previous six pages as your basic units of musical currency. However, that still provides you with a fairly basic palette from which to draw. In fact, to allow you to read and play all possible rhythms you need greater flexibility than can be achieved simply by halving or doubling note values. What for example, would you do, if you wanted to play a note that lasted for THREE beats? Using the values you already know this would not be possible. Similarly, what if you wanted to sustain a note across the bar line? Or even "play" a silence at a given time? All of these are valid musical needs which can be achieved using DOTS, TIES and RESTS.

DOTS AND TIES

Any of the standard note types can be followed by a dot. This has the effect of lengthening that note by half of its value. For example, a minim followed by a dot – referred to as a DOTTED MINIM – has a value of three crotchet beats.

♩. = 3 CROTCHET BEATS

♩. = 1 ¹/₂ CROTCHET BEATS

♪. = ³/₄ OF A CROTCHET BEAT

Exactly the same effect can also be achieved using a curved line known as a TIE. This can be used to link together notes of different values, creating one note whose value is that of the two notes combined. For example, a minim tied to crotchet also has a value of three crotchet beats (2 + 1 beats = 3 beats).

= 3 CROTCHET BEATS

Either of these two approaches are legitimate in written music and can be used interchangeably. However, a crucial difference is that ties can be used to sustain notes across the bar line. In the first staff shown below, the fourth crotchet of the first bar is tied to the minim at the start of the second bar. This has the effect of giving the crotchet a value of three beats. The minim itself is not played. This is a crucial point to remember: the second note in a tied pair is NEVER played under any circumstances, its value is merely added to that of the first tied note.

When ties are written they always join the notes at the head. If the stem points downward the tie is above the note; if the stem points upward, the tie begins below the note.

You can hear the effect of dots and ties on track 2/15 of the CD. In the second example, you will see that there is no difference between the dotted minim and the crotchet tied to the minim – both are sustained for three beats. ▶ 2/15

ONE   ONE   ONE   ONE   TWO   THREE   ONE   ONE

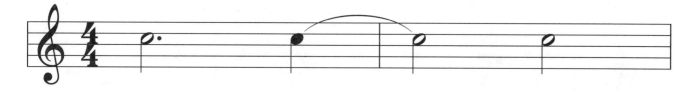

ONE   TWO   THREE   ONE   TWO   THREE   ONE   TWO

USING RESTS IN WRITTEN MUSIC

It may seem strange at first, but a vitally important element of any type of music is silence. Without silence all music would merely be a continous sound. Musical notation has specific instructions for how long periods of silence – known as RESTS – should be shown. Each of the note types you have already encountered has its own associated rest. The most commonly used rests are shown in the panel on the right. It's especially worth noting the difference between the semibreve and minim rests as these can often confuse beginners: the semibreve rest always hangs FROM the fourth line; the minim rest always sits ON the third line.

SPOTTING THE DIFFERENCE

In practice, a rest can sometimes be quite difficult to perceive, especially below the value of a quaver, where the difference between a rest and the natural pause that automatically occurs when moving from one note to another may be hard to discern.

To hear the effect of a crotchet rest, listen to the two examples shown below. The difference is that on the second staff, each of the minims has been replaced with a crotchet and a crotchet rest. This means that in the first bar of the second staff, the third note sustains for just one beat rather than two – as you would imagine if you replaced a minim with a crotchet. NOTHING, however, is played on the fourth beat. The same is true for the second beat of the second bar: it is also rested.

▶ 2 / 16

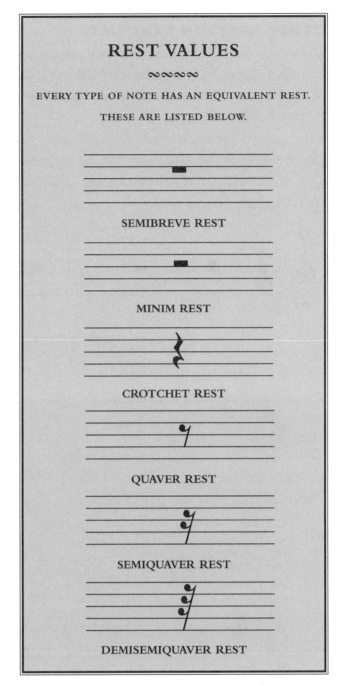

REST VALUES

∼∼∼∼

EVERY TYPE OF NOTE HAS AN EQUIVALENT REST.
THESE ARE LISTED BELOW.

SEMIBREVE REST

MINIM REST

CROTCHET REST

QUAVER REST

SEMIQUAVER REST

DEMISEMIQUAVER REST

ONE   ONE   ONE   TWO   ONE   TWO   ONE   AND   ONE

ONE   ONE   ONE   (TWO)   ONE   (TWO)   ONE AND ONE

OTHER RESTS IN PRACTICE

The first bar below contains a minim rest – it lasts for two crotchet beats. Thus, if you count out the rhythm of the piece it should sound like this: ONE-SILENCE-SILENCE-ONE.

The second bar begins with a beamed group of three quavers followed by a quaver rest and a minim. The count will be ONE-AND-TWO-(SILENT "AND")-ONE-AND-TWO-AND.

> ### RESTING IN BARS
> ∞∞∞∞
> WHEN YOU TOTAL THE NOTE VALUES WITHIN A BAR A REST HAS THE SAME VALUE AS THE NOTE IT REPLACES. FOR EXAMPLE, A BAR MADE UP FROM A MINIM, A CROTCHET AND A CROTCHET REST STILL ADDS UP TO FOUR BEATS.

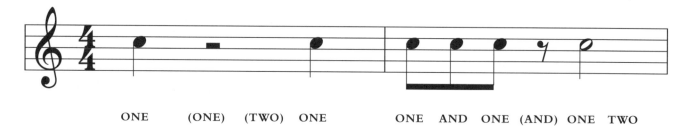

ONE   (ONE) (TWO) ONE   ONE AND ONE (AND) ONE TWO

▶ 2 / 17

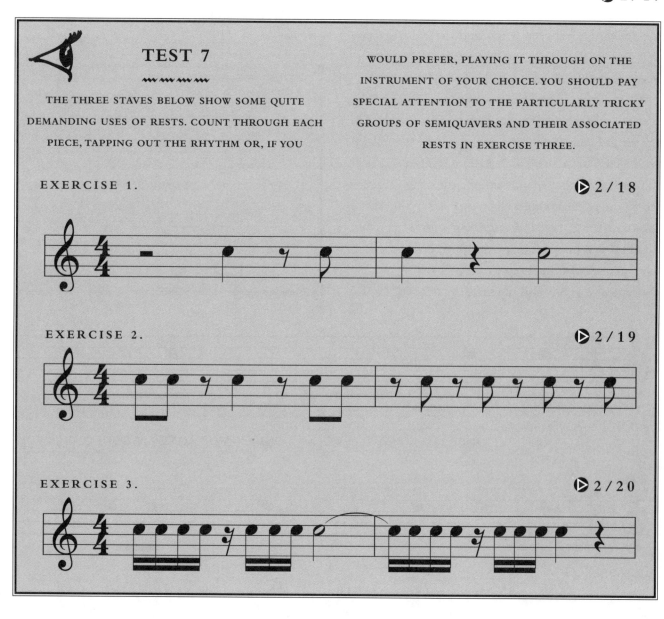

TEST 7
〰〰 〰〰 〰〰 〰〰

THE THREE STAVES BELOW SHOW SOME QUITE DEMANDING USES OF RESTS. COUNT THROUGH EACH PIECE, TAPPING OUT THE RHYTHM OR, IF YOU WOULD PREFER, PLAYING IT THROUGH ON THE INSTRUMENT OF YOUR CHOICE. YOU SHOULD PAY SPECIAL ATTENTION TO THE PARTICULARLY TRICKY GROUPS OF SEMIQUAVERS AND THEIR ASSOCIATED RESTS IN EXERCISE THREE.

EXERCISE 1.   ▶ 2 / 18

EXERCISE 2.   ▶ 2 / 19

EXERCISE 3.   ▶ 2 / 20

BRINGING PITCH AND TIME TOGETHER

In all the examples you have seen so far in lesson, the element of pitch has been deliberately ignored in favour of concentrating exclusively on rhythm. Now it's time to re-acquaint yourself with the note names that you learned during the first lesson. This will give you the opportunity to read through your first "real" piece of music.

Below you will see the music for a children's tune known the world over, "This Old Man". Begin by marking down the names of the individual notes – by all means write them on the book itself, although it's a good idea to use a pencil in case you make an error. Secondly, write out the beat value of all the notes and then tap out the rhythm of the entire tune.

Once you have done this you can play or sing the piece from the start. To make things a little easier the music has been written so that it can be played on the white notes of a piano – you don't need to worry about the enharmonic notes. ▶ 2 / 21

NOTES ON THE TREBLE CLEF

∞∞∞

IF YOU HAVEN'T YET MANAGED TO LEARN THE NAMES OF THE NOTES ON THE TREBLE STAFF BY HEART, HERE IS CRIB THAT WILL HELP YOU GET THROUGH THE EXAMPLE SHOWN BELOW. SEE IF YOU CAN DO THE FINAL TESTS OVER THE PAGE WITHOUT HAVING TO REFER TO IT.

TEST 8

〰〰〰〰〰

COMPLETE THE FOLLOWING FIVE EXERCISES IN THE SAME MANNER AS THE PREVIOUS EXAMPLE. IF YOU ARE SINGING THESE EXERCISES, A PROBLEM YOU MAY FACE IS THE LACK OF A REFERENCE NOTE FROM WHICH TO START. ONE OF THE KEYS TO SIGHT READING IS AN APPRECIATION OF THE PITCHES IN RELATION TO ONE ANOTHER. IF YOU TAKE THE FIRST EXAMPLE, ALTHOUGH IT STARTS ON MIDDLE C, YOUR OWN REFERENCE NOTE CAN BE ANYTHING AT ALL. THE ONLY THING YOU NEED TO KNOW IS THAT THE SECOND NOTE – "F" – IS THREE NOTES HIGHER AND COUNT UP UNTIL YOU REACH THE NOTE. IN TIME THESE INTERVALS WILL BECOME INSTINCTIVE. BEGIN BY WRITING OUT THE NOTE NAMES.

EXERCISE 1. ▶ 2/22

EXERCISE 2. ▶ 2/23

EXERCISE 3. ▶ 2/24

EXERCISE 4. ▶ 2/25

EXERCISE 5. ▶ 2/26

TEST 9

THIS IS A MORE DEMANDING LISTENING TEST. TRACK 2/27 ON THE CD CONTAINS A SINGLE BAR OF MUSIC REPEATED FOUR TIMES. BELOW YOU CAN SEE FOUR BARS OF MUSIC, ALL OF WHICH ARE VERY SLIGHTLY DIFFERENT. YOUR TASK IS TO WORK OUT WHICH OF THE STAVES MATCHES THE MUSIC ON THE CD. THE BEST APPROACH IS TO WORK OUT THE EXAMPLES FIRST AND THEN PLAY THE TRACK ON THE CD TO SEE WHICH IS CORRECT.

▶ 2 / 27

STAFF A.

STAFF B.

STAFF C.

STAFF D.

TEST 10

LOOK AT THE TWO BARS OF MUSIC BELOW – THERE IS SOMETHING WRONG WITH EACH ONE. TRY TO IDENTIFY WHAT THE MISTAKES ARE AND MAKE SOME SUGGESTIONS AS TO HOW THEY MAY BE CORRECTED. A CLUE CAN BE FOUND IN THE TIME SIGNATURE.

TIME OUT: SUMMARY OF LESSON 2

∼∼∼∼

HERE IS A SUMMARY OF THE PRINCIPLE POINTS OF THIS LESSON. IF THERE IS ANYTHING LISTED BELOW THAT YOU ARE NOT SURE ABOUT YOU SHOULD REVIEW THE LAST 12 PAGES BEFORE GOING ON TO LESSON 3.

- CROTCHET BEATS AND FOUR-FOUR TIME
- SEMIBREVE AND MINIM NOTE VALUES
- QUAVERS AND THEIR SUB-DIVISIONS
- THE COMPONENTS OF A NOTE
- THE EFFECT OF DOTTING A NOTE

- THE RULES APPLYING TO TIED NOTES
- THE RESTS ASSOCIATED WITH EACH NOTE TYPE
- CALCULATING BAR VALUES
- AN ABILITY TO SIGHT READ SIMPLE EXAMPLES OF RHYTHM AND PITCH

LESSON 3:

Keys and Scales

A scale is a sequence of related notes. There are many different types of scale, but what makes each one unique is the pattern of intervals each one follows from the starting note – referred to as the ROOT or TONIC – to that same note played an octave higher. Each scale has a key which it takes from the name of the root note.

THE MAJOR SCALE

The most commonly used scale is called a MAJOR scale. You can hear it if you play the white notes on a piano from C to C. The sequence of notes can be either ascending or descending – that is they start from the lowest note or the highest note respectively. Each of the ånotes of the scale are referred to as a degree, from the lowest note to the highest note. They are usually written out using Roman numerals. The scale of C major is shown at the foot of the page, along with its note names and scale degrees. The final degree, which takes the scale back to its starting point, is optionally referred to as either VIII or I.

A piece of music that uses the notes taken from a C major scale is referred to as being IN THE KEY OF C MAJOR.

The intervals between each note of the major scale can be described in terms of semitones and tones. As you have already seen, a semitone is the interval between any two adjacent notes – thus the movement from the notes B to C is a semitone. However, if you look at a piano keyboard, you will see that the distance between some of the white notes is two semitones. For example, C and D are separated by the black note C♯/D♭. To refresh your memory, an interval of two semitones is a tone.

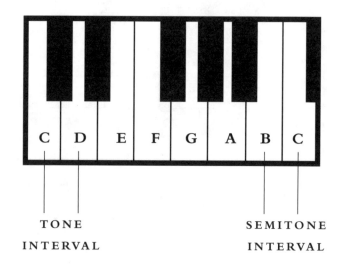

TONE
INTERVAL   SEMITONE
                           INTERVAL

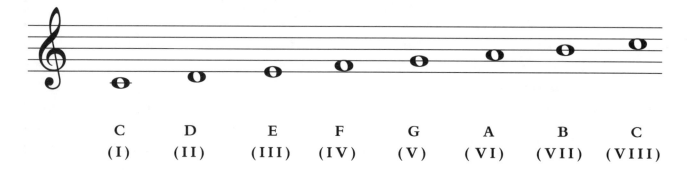

C	D	E	F	G	A	B	C
(I)	(II)	(III)	(IV)	(V)	(VI)	(VII)	(VIII)

MAJOR SCALE INTERVALS

The pattern of intervals between the notes that make up the C major scale are shown below. The intervals that link together the eight degrees are TONE–TONE–SEMITONE–TONE–TONE–TONE–SEMITONE respectively. It is this set of intervals that defines a major scale. Any scale that does NOT have those exact intervals cannot be called a major scale.

If you listen to the C major scale played on any musical instrument you will recognize its familiar sound immediately.   ▶ 3 / 1

> ## TONES OR STEPS?
>
> ∞∽∞∽
>
> IN SOME MUSIC BOOKS YOU MAY COME ACROSS THE TERMS "STEP" AND "HALF-STEP" USED WHEN DISCUSSING INTERVALS. ALTHOUGH THE MAJORITY OF BRITISH MUSICIANS AND TEACHERS USE THE MORE COMMONLY ACCEPTED TERMINOLOGY OF TONES AND SEMITONES, STEPS AND HALF-STEPS ARE PREDOMINANT IN AMERICA.

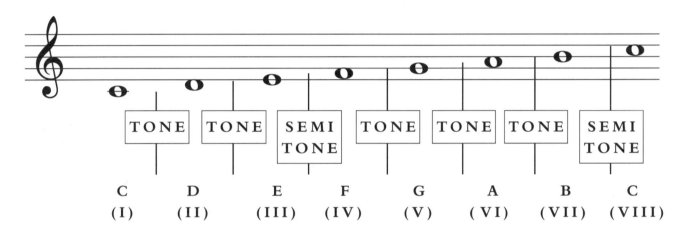

MAJOR SCALE IN G

It is possible to create major scales on every one of the twelve different notes of an octave. For example, if the tonic is moved up to the note G, the same set of tone and semitone intervals can be used to produce the scale of G major. In this instance, you can see from the staff below that the interval between the sixth and seventh degrees means that we must use a black note to make the correct scale. Thus the note F♯ is used. If the note were left as plain F, the interval between the sixth and seventh degrees would only be a semitone and thus the scale would not be correct – this would similarly corrupt the interval between the seventh and eighth degrees.

Although the pitch of F♯ is the same as G♭, in the context of the key of G, the enharmonic note MUST be named F♯ so that a note appears on every line or space in the scalar sequence. You will see why this is so significant when we reach the section on key signatures.   ▶ 3 / 2

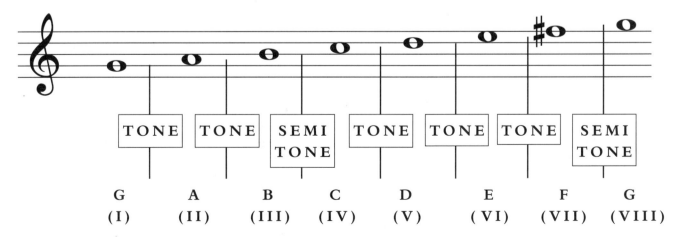

MAJOR SCALE IN F

Using the same major-scale intervals, a scale that starts on an F requires the note B♭ on the third line.

Once again, positioning the note A♯ in the second space would be wrong, even though the pitch of both notes is the same.

▶ 3 / 3

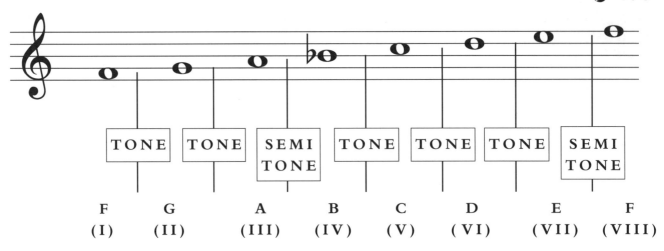

| TONE | TONE | SEMI TONE | TONE | TONE | TONE | SEMI TONE |

F (I)   G (II)   A (III)   B (IV)   C (V)   D (VI)   E (VII)   F (VIII)

KEY SIGNATURES

You have just seen major scales in the keys of C, G and F. In each case, the tonic provided the scale with it KEY SIGNATURE. What this means in practice is NOT that a piece a music in a given key can only use notes from that scale, but that unless otherwise shown the note names given to each space and letter are used throughout the piece. This is straightforward in the key of C major as it does not use any sharps or flats. However, G major requires the use of a single sharp.

Given that the seventh degree of G major is F♯, you could imagine that a piece of music written in G would be heavily peppered with sharp symbols throughout. However, the very fact that the music is in the key of G means that every note on the fifth line of the staff will be F♯. Consequently, the sharp doesn't need to be written out each time, but can be defined by positioning the sharp symbol at the beginning of the clef. Once this becomes a familiar sight you will immediately know that any piece of music with one sharp after the clef is in the key of G, and also that all

references to the note F should be played as F♯. This is a reason why the note MUST be called F♯ rather than G♭ – if it were not, the scale and key of G would have no Fs, but two Gs (G and G♭) which could only be distinguished if every single occurrence of G was somehow marked as a flat or a natural.

Key signatures are used on all clefs. Here is F shown on both treble and bass clefs.

G MAJOR (TREBLE)   G MAJOR (BASS)

Although the key signature marks the sharp on the fifth line of the staff, it is an instruction that EVERY occurrence of F – even on ledger lines – is interpreted as an F♯.

▶ 3 / 4

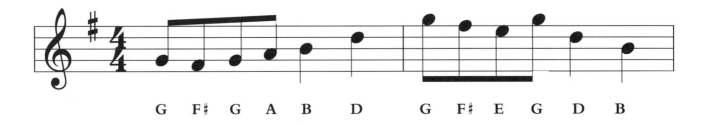

G   F♯   G   A   B   D   G   F♯   E   G   D   B

F WITH A SINGLE FLAT

The same approach applies to the flats. The example below shows a single flat on the third line, indicating that the music is in the key of F. Thus, every note appearing on the third line of the staff should be played as a B♭ NOT B. For music written in the key of F on the bass clef, the flat symbol appears on the second line.

▶ 3 / 5   F MAJOR (TREBLE)   F MAJOR (BASS)

F   B♭   A   B♭   B♭   F   E   D   F   B♭   A   B♭   C   D   B♭

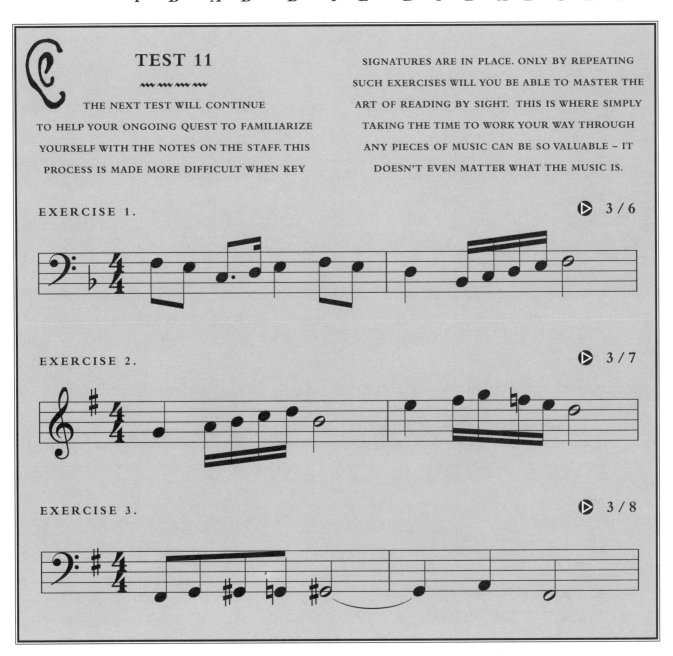

TEST 11

〜〜〜 〜〜〜

THE NEXT TEST WILL CONTINUE TO HELP YOUR ONGOING QUEST TO FAMILIARIZE YOURSELF WITH THE NOTES ON THE STAFF. THIS PROCESS IS MADE MORE DIFFICULT WHEN KEY SIGNATURES ARE IN PLACE. ONLY BY REPEATING SUCH EXERCISES WILL YOU BE ABLE TO MASTER THE ART OF READING BY SIGHT. THIS IS WHERE SIMPLY TAKING THE TIME TO WORK YOUR WAY THROUGH ANY PIECES OF MUSIC CAN BE SO VALUABLE – IT DOESN'T EVEN MATTER WHAT THE MUSIC IS.

EXERCISE 1.   ▶ 3 / 6

EXERCISE 2.   ▶ 3 / 7

EXERCISE 3.   ▶ 3 / 8

EVOLVING KEY SIGNATURES

So far we have only looked at two alternatives to a key signature of C major: G major which has one sharp (F♯), and F major which has one flat (B♭). However, it is possible to build major scales from any of the other notes by following the unique pattern of intervals that defines the major scale.

As you will shortly discover, the time signatures for all of the major scales can be recognized from the number of sharps or flats shown at the beginning of the staff. The number and position of the sharps and flats on each new scale follows a very specific simple mathematical pattern.

PATTERN OF SHARPS

You have already seen that in moving from a scale of C major to G major – the fifth degree of the C major scale – the new key signature features one sharp. If we continue this process you will quickly see the gradual emergence of a clear pattern.

Continuing movements along the fifth degree, the major scale that begins on the fifth degree of G major will have a tonic – and hence key signature – of D. If you project the major scale intervals shown on page 35 from the note D, you will discover that TWO sharps are needed to play the scale correctly. The F♯ from our previous scale is still there, but this time a

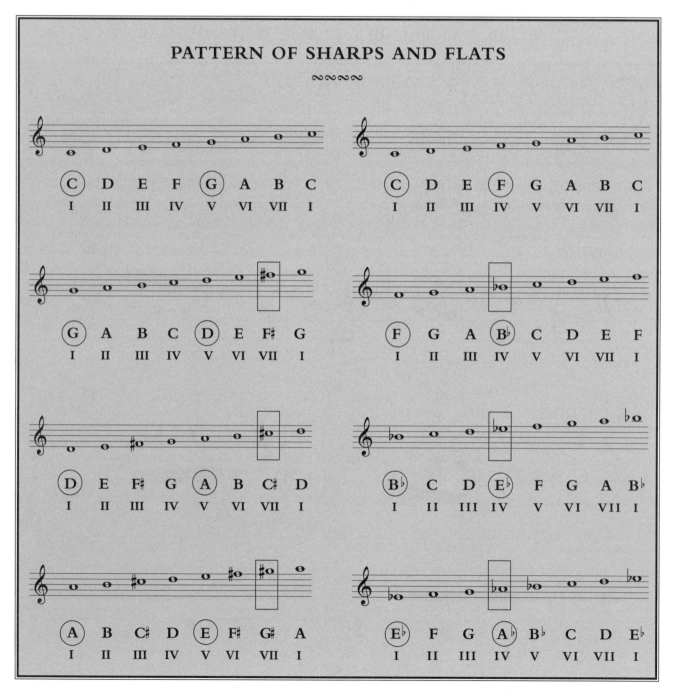

PATTERN OF SHARPS AND FLATS

second sharp exists on the seventh degree of the new scale. Thus, the key signature of D major has TWO SHARPS – F♯ and C♯.

Let's now take this approach one step further by building a scale from the fifth degree of D major. This time the tonic will be A. To build an A major scale using the correct intervals requires the use of THREE sharps. Again, the sharps from the previous scale – F♯ and C♯ – are still present, but, this time a third sharp is added, AGAIN on the seventh degree of the scale, this time G♯.

This process of adding a sharp to the seventh degree of each new scale built on the fifth degree of another can be continued indefinitely, although in practice rarely cycles beyond the key of F♯, which has six sharps. This relationship is shown on the left-hand column of the panel on the opposite page.

THE PATTERN OF FLATS

The same kind of principle can also be applied to the key signatures that use flats. You have already seen that moving between the keys of C major and F major produces a key signature that requires a single flat – the note B♭. Think of this as being a new scale built this time from the FOURTH degree of C major (rather than the fifth degree that was used to create the key signatures showing sharps).

Start by building a new major scale from the fourth degree of F major. Projecting the same pattern of intervals from the note B♭, the new scale comprises the notes B♭, C, D, E♭, F, G and A. You can see the same kind of pattern beginning to emerge. Each time a major scale is built from the FOURTH degree, a flat is added to the fourth degree of the resulting scale.

Taking it one step further, the fourth degree of B♭ is E♭. Projecting the major scale intervals from E♭ major requires the addition of a flat on the fourth degree, thus the new scale is E♭, F, G, A♭. B♭, C, D, E♭. This set of relationships is shown in the right-hand column in the panel across the page.

If you find any of this section difficult or daunting, don't be too concerned for now. This is one of the few areas of maths-oriented theory covered in the book. In practice, the use of key signatures is much more straightforward.

TEST 12

ANSWER THE FOLLOWING 20 QUESTIONS:

1. WHICH MAJOR KEY SIGNATURE USES NO SHARPS OR FLATS?

2. THE KEY OF F USES THE NOTE A♮. IS THIS TRUE?

3. NAME THE FOURTH DEGREE OF G MAJOR.

4. ARE THERE TWO SHARPS OR THREE IN THE KEY OF D MAJOR?

5. THE INTERVAL BETWEEN THE NOTES E AND F COULD BE CALLED A TONE. IS THIS TRUE?

6. WHICH MAJOR KEY USES FIVE SHARPS?

7. THE SIXTH DEGREE OF D MAJOR IS THE SAME NOTE AS THE SECOND DEGREE OF A MAJOR. IS THIS TRUE?

8. IN THE KEY OF G MAJOR ON THE BASS CLEF, THE SHARP SYMBOL APPEARS ON THE FOURTH SPACE. IS THIS TRUE?

9. THE FIRST SEVEN NOTES OF THIS MAJOR SCALE HAVE BEEN JUMBLED UP – E, A, B, C♯, F♯, D, G♯. PUT THEM IN SEQUENCE AND NAME THE SCALE.

10. NAME THE SEVENTH DEGREE OF A MAJOR.

11. WOULD IT ALWAYS BE ACCURATE TO DESCRIBE THE INTERVAL BETWEEN THE NOTES G AND C AS FIVE SEMITONES?

12. HOW MANY SHARPS OR FLATS DOES THE KEY OF A♭ MAJOR REQUIRE?

13. IN THE KEY SIGNATURE OF E, THE FOUR SHARPS APPEAR ON THE SAME LINES ON BOTH THE TREBLE CLEF AND THE BASS CLEF. IS THIS TRUE?

14. IS THE THIRD DEGREE OF C MAJOR AND THE SIX DEGREE OF G MAJOR THE SAME NOTE?

15. F♯ AND A♭ HAVE THE SAME PITCH. IS THIS TRUE?

16. IS B♭ THE SAME NOTE AS A♯?

17. THE MAJOR KEYS OF C, G, D AND A ALL HAVE AT LEAST ONE SHARP ON THE SEVENTH DEGREE. IS THIS TRUE?

18. HOW MANY FLATS DOES THE KEY OF E♭ REQUIRE?

19. B♭ MAJOR USES TWO FLATS. WHICH ARE THEY?

20. THE SIXTH DEGREES OF E♭ AND D ARE ONE SEMITONE APART. IS THIS TRUE?

THE CIRCLE OF FIFTHS

The full pattern of relationships between the scales starting on both the fifth and fourth degrees can be depicted as a wheel. This is known as the CIRCLE OF FIFTHS.

The notes are laid out so that when counting clockwise, each subsequent letter is the FIFTH DEGREE of the previous scale. By starting at the top of the circle on C, each step you count clockwise adds a sharp to the key signature of that note. Moreover, the additional sharp is always on the seventh degree of the new scale.

The converse is also true. If you count in an anti-clockwise direction, each subsequent letter is a fifth degree DOWN from the tonic of the previous scale. In practice, this makes the tonic for the new scale the same as the FOURTH DEGREE of the previous scale. Thus by starting at the top of the circle, each step you count anticlockwise adds a FLAT to the key signature for that note. Each additional flat appears on the fourth degree of the new scale.

The circle of fifths provides a convenient way of memorizing the patterns that create key signatures. It's a good idea to take some time out to learn these

CIRCLE OF FIFTHS (TREBLE CLEF)

off by by heart. It's an absolute necessity if you are to be able to sight read effectively.

The diagram on the left shows the the positioning of sharps and flats on the treble clef. Whilst this is the most commonly used range of notes, you should acquaint yourself with the positions on the bass clef. This is shown below. You might have noticed that the bottom three segments have enharmonic alternatives. The keys of F♯ and G♭ are both used, thus both possibilities are shown. It IS possible to use keys of C♯ and C♭ (seven sharps or flats respectively), but it's far more common to see these keys written as B or D♭.

TIME OUT: SUMMARY OF LESSON 3

∞∞∞∞

- MAJOR SCALE INTERVALS
- KEY SIGNATURES ON THE STAFF
- EVOLVING SCALES FROM THE FIFTH DEGREE
- EVOLVING SCALES FROM THE FOURTH DEGREE
- THE CIRCLE OF FIFTHS ON THE TREBLE CLEF
- THE CIRCLE OF FIFTHS ON THE BASS CLEF

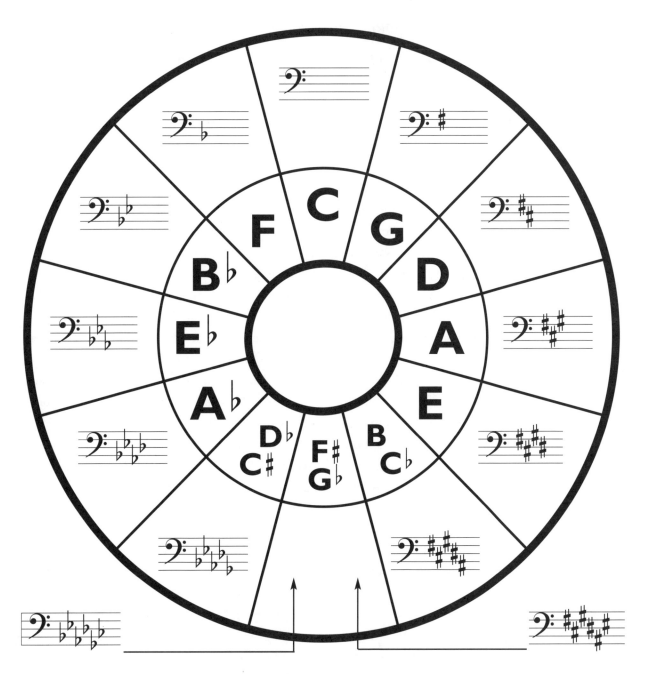

CIRCLE OF FIFTHS (BASS CLEF)

LESSON 4:

Time and Tempo

When notes are written down they are grouped together in small blocks called BARS. Each bar contains a defined number of beats. So far, all of the musical examples you have seen have used the same kind groupings – ones that show four beats in every bar. This is a time signature of four-four, which you will already have seen written at the start of some of the bars of music. There are many other possible time signatures.

TIME SIGNATURES

A four-four beat is much the most commonly used time signature. So frequent is its use that it may be referred to as COMMON TIME. In some cases, instead of the "fractional" time signature being shown at the beginning of the staff, a modified C symbol can be used instead – **C**. This is a symbol that has lingered from the early days of written music. There are, however, many other possible time signatures.

First, though, let us take a look at what those fraction-like numbers that you see at the start of a piece of music really mean. The number at top tells you quite simply how many beats there are in the bar. The number at the bottom indicates the time value of each of those beats. If the bottom number is two, the beat is shown as minims; if it is four the beat is shown as crotchets; if it is eight, the beat is shown as quavers. Whilst it would be possible to show the beat as semi-

breves (with a number 1) or semiquavers (with a number 16) this is very rarely seen in practice.

SIMPLE TIME

Listen to the three bars shown across the page. They are written in time signatures of two-four, three-four, and four-four. As each track plays, notice how the natural emphasis falls on the first beat. It is this emphasis that creates the mood of the track, even though no pitched notes are being played.

Although only one bar of music is shown for each example, tracks 4/1 to 4/3 on the CD play each staff for 16 bars, giving you the opportunity to listen and join in. As you clap, count out the beats, emphasising the word "ONE" each time. The first example repeats the count <u>ONE</u>-TWO. In the second example the count will be <u>ONE</u>-TWO-THREE. Such accenting naturally occurs every two or three beats – you can think four-four time as having two accents, the strongest on ONE and a weaker one of THREE.

Notice how if it were not for these accents the three time signatures would actually sound identical. This is because the TEMPO in each case is identical. The tempo refers to the actual time each crotchet takes to play, which governs the overall speed. Although they are spaced out differently in their respective bars, each crotchet is sustained for exactly the same time.

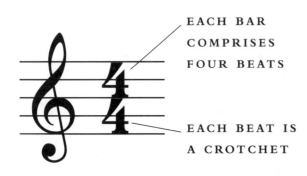

EACH BAR
COMPRISES
FOUR BEATS

EACH BEAT IS
A CROTCHET

CROTCHETS OR QUARTER NOTES?

∾∾∾∾

AS WITH THE TERMINOLOGY RELATING TO TONES AND SEMITONES, IN THE UNITED STATES NOTE VALUES ARE GIVEN ALTERNATIVE NAMES. THE SYSTEM THEY USE IS ARGUABLY SOMEWHAT MORE LOGICAL THAN THE EUROPEAN CONVENTION. INSTEAD OF USING ARCHAIC TERMS THAT DATE BACK TO THE SEVENTEENTH CENTURY, NOTE TYPES ARE SIMPLY REFERRED TO AS FRACTIONS OF A NOTE WORTH FOUR BEATS. HENCE A SEMI BREVE IS KNOWN AS A WHOLE NOTE; A MINIM – TWO BEATS – IS A HALF NOTE, AND SO FORTH. A FULL LIST IS SHOWN ON THE RIGHT.

IT IS WORTHWHILE ACQUAINTING YOURSELF WITH THIS SYSTEM ALONGSIDE THE TRADITIONAL EUROPEAN APPROACH. THE US SYSTEM CAN BE ESPECIALLY USEFUL WHEN WORKING OUT ASPECTS OF TIMING AND RHYTHM, ESPECIALLY THE WAY IN WHICH IT CAN BE RELATED TO THE LOWER FIGURE IN THE TIME SIGNATURE "FRACTION".

WHOLE NOTE (SEMIBREVE)

HALF NOTE (MINIM)

QUARTER NOTE (CROTCHET)

EIGHTH NOTE (QUAVER)

SIXTEENTH NOTE (SEMIQUAVER)

THIRTY-SECOND NOTE (DEMISEMIQUAVER)

BAR OF TWO-FOUR (TWO CROTCHETS)

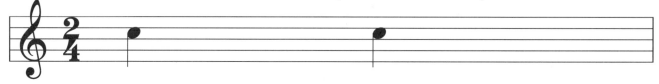

▶ 4 / 1

BAR OF THREE-FOUR (THREE CROTCHETS)

▶ 4 / 2

BAR OF FOUR-FOUR (FOUR CROTCHETS)

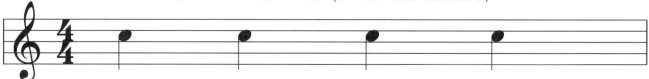

▶ 4 / 3

SIMPLE TIME IN PRACTICE

An ambiguous area worth noting is the question of the difference in practice between a time signature of two-four and four-four. It is clearly possible to count out two bars of two-four as a single bar of four-four. But this rather begs the question of why composers bother to make a distinction between the two.

One of the most common uses for two-four time is in marching music. Here the reasoning is fairly clear if we imagine soldiers on parade marching to the order "LEFT-RIGHT-LEFT-RIGHT". In this case, each complete movement consists of two parts – the left leg followed by the right. Whilst you *could* count it out as "ONE-TWO-THREE-FOUR", the beats fall more naturally into groupings of two. Given that in a bar of four-four there is a weaker emphasis on the third beat than on the first, unless the music itself reflects this emphasis then we can reasonably say that giving it a time signature of four-four would be incorrect. Some cases, however, may be less clear cut and difference can be attributed more to the mood of the music. This illustrates the point that outside of the basic rules, many of the finer shades of music notation are quite discretionary, and can easily be adapted for ease of use or to aid communication – which *is*, after all, the point in writing down music.

MIXED NOTE VALUES IN SIMPLE TIME

In the three staves shown on the previous page you will have noticed that, as always, the total value of the notes within each bar tallies with the top number in the time signature.

Below, is a simple example of a three-four time signature – the nursery tune "Lavender's Blue". Notice when you are counting out the note values that they MUST total three beats. Hence, unlike a bar of four-four time, a note that lasts for an entire bar CANNOT be a semibreve because that is worth four beats. Instead we must use a DOTTED MINIM, which is worth three beats.

This time signature has an unmistakable flavour and is often referred to either as "Waltz Time" or "Triple Time".   **4 / 4**

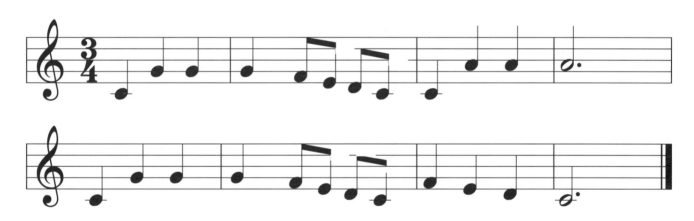

COMPOUND TIME

The three simple time signatures all have beats which are divisible by two. Another kind of time signature is possible with the beats divisible by three. This is known as COMPOUND TIME.

A two-beat bar in simple time with a time signature of two-four can be played as two groups of quavers. In compound time, a two-beat bar with a time signature of six-eight would be played as two groups of three quavers.

Similarly, a three-beat bar can be played as three groups of quavers in a time signature of nine-eight, and a four-beat bar can be played as four groups of quavers in a time signature of twelve-eight.

Three examples of compound time are shown below. Count through each one carefully.

BAR OF SIX-EIGHT (SIX QUAVERS)

▶ 4 / 5

BAR OF NINE-EIGHT (NINE QUAVERS)

▶ 4 / 6

BAR OF TWELVE-EIGHT (TWELVE QUAVERS)

▶ 4 / 7

A MATTER OF EMPHASIS

The way in which notes are emphasised – or how loudly they are played – is extremely important. Without it, music would be both dull and two-dimensional. A clue as to the way individual beats should be emphasised can be found in the way in which the notes are laid out.

The example below shows two bars each with six quavers, hence it has a time signature of 6/8. The first bar is shown as two beamed groups of three, the second as three beamed groups of two. The fact they have been grouped in this way tells us that while the principle emphasis still lies on the first beat, the first bar contains a secondary weaker emphasis on the fourth beat. In the second bar, however, there are two secondary emphases of equal parity that fall on the third and fifth beats. However, such changes in dynamic are subtle and should by no means be viewed as performance instruction, for example, to dramatically increase the volume of the note. We will be coming onto such areas further down the line.

▶ 4 / 8

ASYMMETRIC TIME

There also exists a number of less commonly used times signatures whose numbers are not divisible by two or three. These are known as ASYMMETRIC TIME signature. The most frequent asymmetric times count in fives and sevens, however bars of eleven and thirteen are also sometimes used.

As "unnatural" or complex as some they may sound, even the toughest asymmetric time signature can be viewed more easily as a combination of groups of two, three or four beats.

FIVE-FOUR TIME

The first example below shows two bars with a time signature of of five-four, each bar comprising five crotchets. It is possible to view this time signature as a group of three crotchets followed by a group of two, or vice versa. In this instance we don't have beamed quavers to imply an emphasis so an ACCENT is used instead. This is an instruction to play the note louder by positioning the symbol "∧" above the note (">" can also be positioned above the note or "∨" placed below the note). The first bar can be counted as ONE-TWO-ONE-TWO-THREE. The second is counted as ONE-TWO-THREE-ONE-TWO.

SEVEN-FOUR TIME

The second example has a time signature of seven-four. Again, this can be viewed as a group of three crotchets followed by a group of four, or vice versa. A third alternative not shown on the staff is to count out a group of two, a group of three and then another group of two. For example, ONE-TWO-ONE-TWO-THREE-ONE-TWO.

BARS OF FIVE-FOUR (FIVE CROTCHETS)

▶ 4 / 9

BARS OF SEVEN-FOUR (SEVEN CROTCHETS)

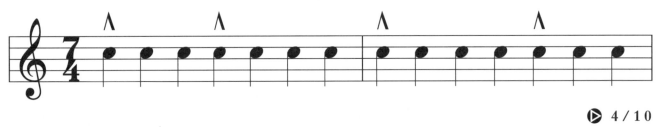

▶ 4 / 10

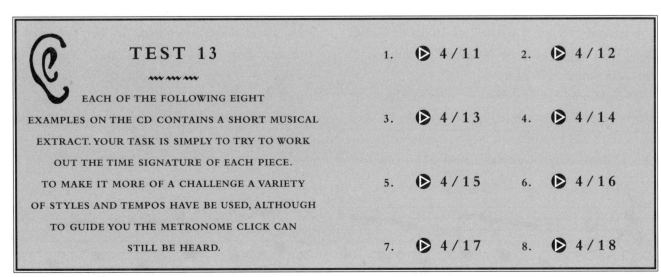

TEST 13

〜〜〜

EACH OF THE FOLLOWING EIGHT EXAMPLES ON THE CD CONTAINS A SHORT MUSICAL EXTRACT. YOUR TASK IS SIMPLY TO TRY TO WORK OUT THE TIME SIGNATURE OF EACH PIECE. TO MAKE IT MORE OF A CHALLENGE A VARIETY OF STYLES AND TEMPOS HAVE BE USED, ALTHOUGH TO GUIDE YOU THE METRONOME CLICK CAN STILL BE HEARD.

1. ▶ 4 / 11   2. ▶ 4 / 12

3. ▶ 4 / 13   4. ▶ 4 / 14

5. ▶ 4 / 15   6. ▶ 4 / 16

7. ▶ 4 / 17   8. ▶ 4 / 18

TEST 14

BELOW YOU WILL SEE EIGHT SINGLE BARS OF MUSIC. IN EACH INSTANCE THE TIME SIGNATURE HAS BEEN REMOVED FROM THE STAFF. BY TOTALLING THE VARIOUS NOTE VALUES WITHIN EACH BAR YOU SHOULD BE ABLE TO WORK OUT THE CORRECT TIME SIGNATURE. AS AN ADDITIONAL TEST, WRITE DOWN THE NAMES OF ALL THE NOTES AS WELL AS THE MAJOR KEY SIGNATURES. YOU CAN REFER TO THE "CIRCLE OF FIFTHS" AT THE END OF LESSON THREE IF YOU NEED TO REFRESH YOUR MEMORY ON THE SUBJECT.

1.

2.

3.

4.

5.

6.

CHANGING TIMES

It's perfectly feasible for time signatures to change within a single piece of music. The notation for such occurrences is quite simple – when it happens the new time signature is placed at the start of the new bar-line. From that point onwards this new time signature remains unchanged until either the piece is completed or a further change in time signature is instructed. The piece shown below features three changes in meter. On the CD it is played over a metronome click so you can hear the change more effectively. ▶ 4 / 19

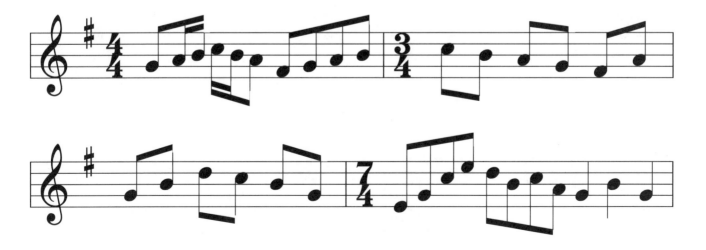

TEMPOS

The speed at which a piece of music is played is referred to as the TEMPO. In written music this can be shown in two different ways: it can either be in the form of a generalized written instruction — "fast" or "very fast", for example — or in terms of how many beats can be played in a minute. This latter instruction appears at the start of the music and is shown as a note-type followed by a numeric value.

$$\text{♩} = 100$$

The example above indicates that one hundred crotchet beats are to be played every minute.

It is possible to measure this figure in a number of different ways. Traditionally, musicians and composers have used a pyramid-shaped mechanical device called a METRONOME. This can be manually set so that it provides an audible click at a specified tempo. Invented in around 1812 by a Dutchman named Dietrich Winkler, the idea of the metronome was copied, modified and patented in 1815 by Johann Maelzel who, although later sued by Winkler, became the name most commonly associated with the device. So much so, in fact, that it became widely known as the "Maelzel Metronome" and, to the present day,

some written music can be seen to show the letters "M.M." alongside the time value.

$$\text{M.M.} = 100$$

In recent times, many modern musicians have turned to the electronic drum machine or MIDI sequencer to produce the same effect. As such, the terminology "BEATS PER MINUTE" or "B.P.M." used by such equipment has become more widely used. Indeed the growth of "DJ culture" and the widespread popularity of electronic dance music has brought the term into popular vocabulary.

Whilst this figure is extremely precise, in practice it is often used as a general guide rather than fixed value. Although most classical compositions would show such a figure the music, it is fair to say that few musicians or conductors have such perfect timing skills as to know these values instinctively. Some compositions acknowledge these vagaries by prefixing the beat value with the Italian word "*circa*", meaning "about". This is usually shown as "c.".

WATCHING THE NOTE TYPE

Most metronome marks — a name sometimes given to these beat values — are shown in terms of crotchet values, but these can alter depending on the music. Look

SIMPLE TO COMPOUND

∞∾∾∞

THE NOTION OF ATTRIBUTING A FIXED TIME VALUE TO A NOTE TYPE CAN ALSO BE FOUND WHEN A PIECE OF MUSIC CHANGES ITS TIME SIGNATURE, MOST TYPICALLY WHEN SHIFTING BETWEEN SIMPLE TIME AND COMPOUND TIME, SUCH AS BETWEEN 3/4 AND 6/8. IN THE EXAMPLE SHOWN BELOW, TO KEEP THE TEMPO CONSISTENT IT MUST BE SHOWN THAT THE TIME VALUE OF THE CROTCHET IN SIMPLE TIME (3/4) IS IDENTICAL TO THE VALUE OF A DOTTED CROTCHET IN COMPOUND TIME (6/8). THIS CAN BE ACHIEVED SIMPLY EQUATING THE CROTCHET AND DOTTED CROTCHET DIRECTLY ABOVE THE BAR LINE AT WHICH THE CHANGE IN TIME SIGNATURE COMES INTO EFFECT. YOU CAN HEAR THE DIFFERENCE THIS MAKES ON THE CD. THE FIRST EXAMPLE IS PLAYED AS SHOWN BELOW – THE SECOND IS PLAYED AS IF THE MARK HAD NOT BEEN MADE DIRECTLY ABOVE THE BAR-LINE. ▶ 4/20

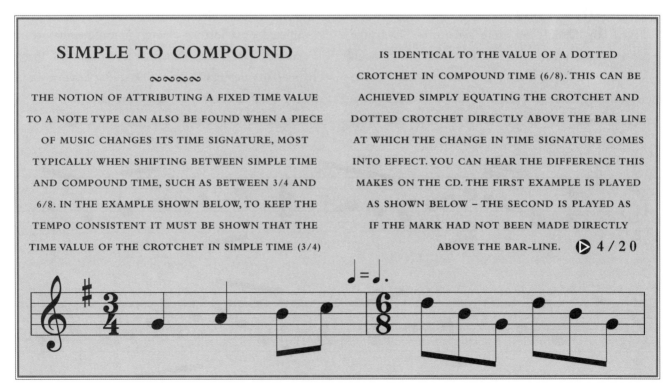

TEMPO MARKS

∞∞∞∞

ITALIAN NAME	DESCRIPTION	BPM
GRAVE	VERY SLOW, SERIOUS	BELOW 40
LENTO	SLOW	40-55
ADAGIO	SLOW (LITERALLY, AT EASE)	55-75
ANDANTE	WALKING SPEED	75-105
MODERATO	MODERATE SPEED	105-120
ALLEGRO	FAST (LITERALLY, CHEERFUL)	120-150
VIVACE	LIVELY	150-170
PRESTO	VERY FAST	170-210
PRESTISSIMO	AS FAST AS POSSIBLE	ABOVE 210

at the two metronome marks shown below. If you were to muddle them up, the music you played would sound very different – one hundred minims per minute means an equivalent speed of two hundred crotchets per minute.

$$\text{♩} = 100 \qquad \text{𝅗𝅥} = 100$$

WRITTEN TEMPO MARKS

A great deal of classical music is deliberately specified in terms of a general tempo. These instructions have traditionally been shown in their original Italian names, which has meant that for several centuries, classical musicians throughout the world have had

to acquaint themselves with a modest vocabulary of foreign terms.

The list in the panel at the top of the page shows a wide selection of these terms, which are known as TEMPO MARKS. Alongside the translation you will find an approximate range in beats per minute. As you can see, the player or conductor has considerable scope for their own interpretation – after all, a piece played *Andante* is likely to sound very different when played at 75 B.P.M. to a performance executed at the relatively brisk 105 B.P.M.

A further traditional use for tempo marks – and one which has caused a degree of confusion in the past – is that they are also sometimes used to indicate the character of the music, that is, the mood in which it should be played.

TIME OUT: SUMMARY OF LESSON 4

∞∞∞∞

HERE IS A SUMMARY OF THE MAJOR POINTS SHOWN IN THIS LESSON. THERE IS SOME COMPLEX MATERIAL IN THIS SECTION SO YOU SHOULD SPEND SOME TIME REVIEWING IT BEFORE GOING ON TO LESSON 5.

- THE COMPONENTS OF THE TIME SIGNATURE
- TWO-FOUR SIMPLE TIME
- THREE-FOUR SIMPLE TIME
- FOUR-FOUR SIMPLE TIME
- COMPOUND TIME

- EMPHASIS OF THE BEAT
- FIVE-FOUR ASYMMETRIC TIME
- SEVEN-FOUR ASYMMETRIC TIME
- METRONOME MARKS
- TEMPO MARKS

LESSON 5:

Minor Scales

You have already seen how the major scale is constructed from a fixed pattern of seven intervals. There is another other series of scales which is also very commonly used — these are known as the MINOR SCALES. There are three distinct types of minor scale, each with their own fixed set of intervals. Like the major scale, they are all built from a series of eight notes between the root and the octave.

WHAT IS A MINOR SCALE?

Just as a piece of music written in a major key has a certain characteristic flavour, so too does music written in a minor key. It is over-simplistic to generalize, but pieces of music that strike you as being mournful or melancholic are likely to have been written in minor keys. Contrast, for example, "The Wedding March", which is written in a major key with "The Funeral March" which is in a minor key.   ▶ 5 / 1

THE NATURAL MINOR SCALE

Unlike the major scale, whose pattern of intervals always remain the same, there are three different types of minor scale, each with its own subtly different characteristic. They are the NATURAL MINOR (sometimes called the RELATIVE MINOR), the HARMONIC MINOR and the MELODIC MINOR. All of the minor scales have one common difference from a major scale in that the 3rd degree is always lowered by a semitone. The differences among the minor scales revolve around movements of the 6th and 7th degrees.

The pattern of intervals between the notes that make up the NATURAL MINOR scale are shown below. The intervals are TONE–SEMITONE–TONE–TONE–SEMITONE–TONE–TONE. To form a natural minor scale from a major scale, the 3rd, 6th and 7th degrees are lowered by a semitone. On the CD you can hear the scale played ascending (as shown below) and descending – played from the 8th degree down to the 1st.   ▶ 5 / 2

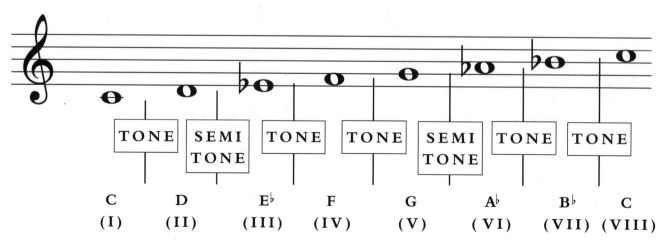

| TONE | SEMI TONE | TONE | TONE | SEMI TONE | TONE | TONE |

| C | D | E♭ | F | G | A♭ | B♭ | C |
| (I) | (II) | (III) | (IV) | (V) | (VI) | (VII) | (VIII) |

RELATIVE MAJORS AND MINORS

Although the pattern of intervals used by a major and natural minor scale are clearly not the same, an interesting relationship between these two types of scale can be seen when a natural minor scale is built from the 6th degree of a major scale. The examples below show C major and A natural minor (the note A is the 6th degree of C major). As you can see, both scales use the same set of notes, although starting from different roots. Play the two scales, or listen to track 5/3 on the CD, to hear the difference.

The relationship between these two scales can be termed in one of two ways: the key of A minor can be described as a RELATIVE MINOR of C major; or the key of C major can be termed a RELATIVE MAJOR of A minor.

▶ 5 / 3

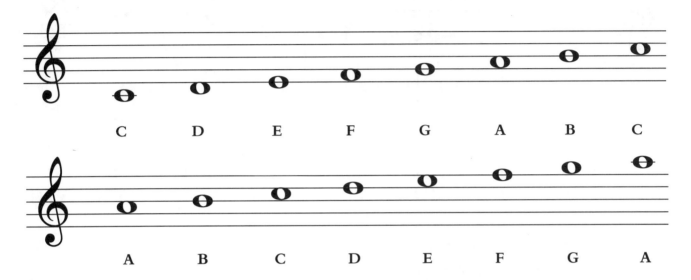

RELATIVE MINORS RELATIONSHIPS AND KEY SIGNATURES

The fixed relationship between the major and minor scales is extremely useful in identifying key signatures. Just as it is possible to tell the key of a piece of music by counting the number of sharps and flats between the clef and the time signature meter, the relationship described above means that the same observations can be made for music written in a minor key.

A list of the most commonly used major-key signatures is shown below along with their relative minor equivalents.

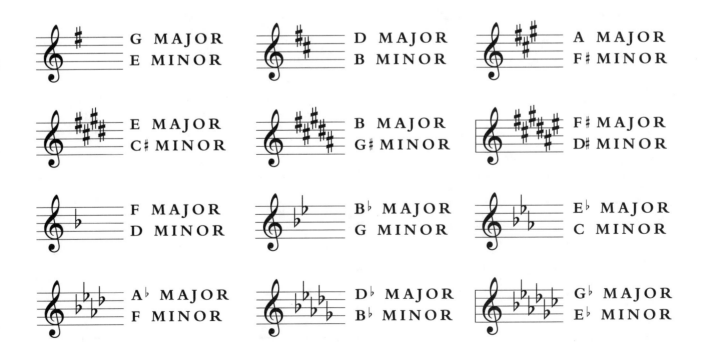

THE HARMONIC MINOR SCALE

The harmonic minor scale differs from the natural minor scale in that the 7th degree is sharpened – it is raised by a semitone. Thus, the pattern of intervals required to create the scale are TONE-SEMITONE-TONE-TONE-SEMITONE-TONE PLUS SEMI-TONE–SEMITONE. Notice that by sharpening the 7th degree the interval between the 6th and 7th degrees is now three semitones.

If you listen to track 5/4 of the CD you can hear C harmonic minor (shown below) played as both ascending and descending scales.   ▶ **5 / 4**

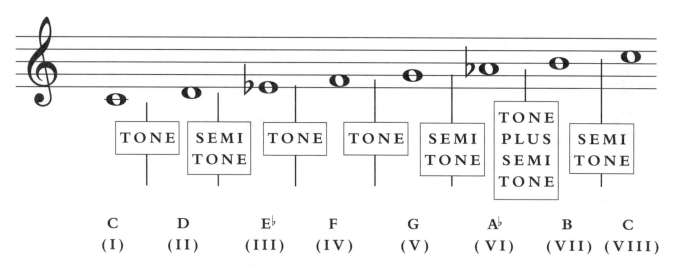

| C | D | E♭ | F | G | A♭ | B | C |
| (I) | (II) | (III) | (IV) | (V) | (VI) | (VII) | (VIII) |

NAMING THE DEGREES

∾∾∾∾

ALL OF THE SO-CALLED DIATONIC SCALES – THE MAJOR AND MINOR SERIES – ARE MADE OF EIGHT INDIVIDUAL NOTES. EACH OF THESE DEGREES CAN BE NAMED. THE FIRST NOTE IS THE <u>TONIC</u>. THE FIFTH DEGREE, AFTER THE TONIC THE MOST IMPORTANT NOTE IN THE SCALE, IS CALLED THE <u>DOMINANT</u>. THE FOURTH DEGREE TAKES THE NAME <u>SUBDOMINANT</u> SINCE IT SHARES THE SAME INTERVAL AS THAT OF THE TONIC AND DOMINANT ONLY COUNTED <u>BENEATH</u> THE TONIC. THE SECOND DEGREE IS THE <u>SUPERTONIC</u>. THIS TERM COMES FROM THE LATIN WORD *SUPER* MEANING "AFTER" – QUITE LOGICAL AS IT FOLLOWS THE TONIC. THE THIRD DEGREE IS THE <u>MEDIANT</u>, SO-CALLED BECAUSE OF ITS POSITION HALF WAY BETWEEN THE TONIC AND THE DOMINANT. THE SIXTH DEGREE IS THE <u>SUBMEDIANT</u>, WHICH HAS THE SAME INTERVAL AS THAT OF THE TONIC AND MEDIANT WHEN COUNTED BENEATH THE TONIC. THE 7TH DEGREE IS THE <u>LEADING NOTE</u>.

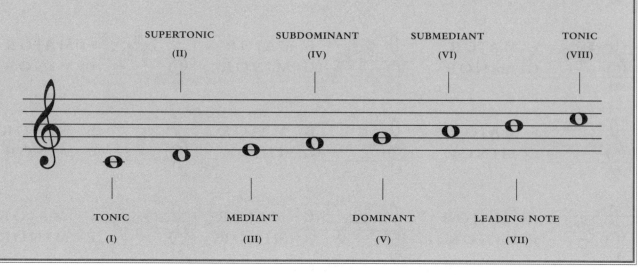

SUPERTONIC (II)   SUBDOMINANT (IV)   SUBMEDIANT (VI)   TONIC (VIII)

TONIC (I)   MEDIANT (III)   DOMINANT (V)   LEADING NOTE (VII)

THE MELODIC MINOR SCALE (ASCENDING)

A problem for melodies that use the harmonic minor scale is in the "difficult" pitch interval of three semitones between the 6th and 7th degrees. To overcome this, the submediant (the 6th degree) can be raised by a semitone to create what is called a MELODIC MINOR scale.

The pattern of intervals that defines a melodic minor scale are TONE–SEMITONE-TONE-TONE-TONE-TONE-SEMITONE.

You can hear the smoothing effect created by "sharpening" the 6th degree of the scale if you listen to track 5/5 of the CD. Contrast the way this scale sounds with the C minor harmonic scale shown at the top of the opposite page.   ▶ **5 / 5**

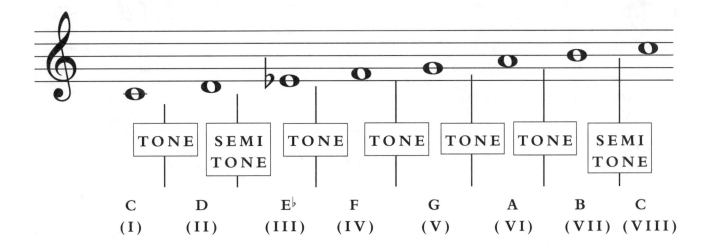

THE MELODIC MINOR SCALE (DESCENDING)

Whilst the majority of melodies written in a minor key make use of the sharpened sixth and seventh notes when ascending – playing UP the scale – this can sound awkward when descending – playing DOWN the scale. The solution to this problem is quite simple. When descending the melodic minor scale you play the unsharpened 6th and 7th notes – these sound far more appropriate. Therefore, whilst the pattern of intervals described above for the

melodic minor is correct when ascending, when descending you have to revert to the notes of the NATURAL MINOR. The pattern of intervals for this descending scale is TONE–TONE–SEMI-TONE–TONE–TONE–SEMITONE–TONE.

You can hear the ascending C melodic minor scale (shown above) on track 5/5 of the CD, followed immediately by the corrected descending scale (shown below).

It is important that you understand the distinction between these two scales.   ▶ **5 / 6**

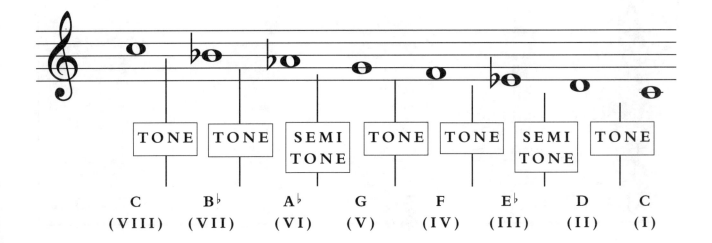

TEST 15

SIX MINOR SCALES ARE SHOWN BELOW. IN EACH CASE AT LEAST TWO OF THE

NOTES HAVE BEEN LEFT OUT. YOUR TASK IS TO WORK OUT THE NAMES OF THE MISSING NOTES. YOU ARE PROVIDED WITH THE NAME OF EACH SCALE. THE ANSWERS ARE ON PAGE 122.

EXERCISE 1. A MELODIC MINOR

EXERCISE 2. E NATURAL MINOR

EXERCISE 3. D HARMONIC MINOR

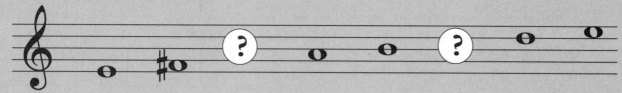

EXERCISE 4. G MELODIC MINOR

EXERCISE 5. B MELODIC MINOR

EXERCISE 6. D MELODIC MINOR

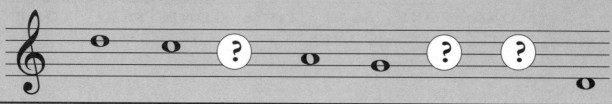

DOUBLE SHARPS AND FLATS

At the moment you are familiar with the use of three of the ACCIDENTALS – the symbols used to raise or lower the pitch. These are the sharp, the flat and the natural. However, in some situations, such as the creation of certain minor scales, it becomes necessary to sharpen a note that has already been sharpened, or flatten a note that has already been flattened. To achieve this you use either a DOUBLE FLAT or a DOUBLE SHARP.

The double flat is shown in written music using this symbol – "♭♭". It has the effect of reducing the pitch of the note by two semitones. A note shown as B♭♭ has the same pitch value as the note A, although it

would be inappropriate to term it "A" in such a context. The double sharp – shown either as "x" or the musical symbol "✗" – works in a similar way, raising the pitch by two semitones.

The example below shows a G♯ melodic minor scale. The key signature of G♯ minor already features a sharpened F. However, this scale requires the 7th degree (F♯) to be sharpened. Thus the note is shown as F✗. Although the note has the same pitch as G, using a key signature of G♯, the "G" space directly about the top line of the staff is already G♯ by default.

To restore the note to its original pitch you simply replace the "double" symbol with either a single sharp or a single flat.

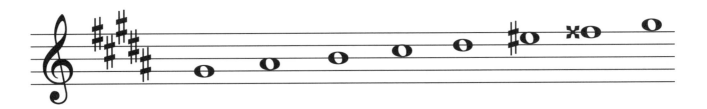

TEST 16

〰〰〰

ON THE CD YOU WILL HEAR EIGHT DIFFERENT MINOR SCALES BEING PLAYED IN A VARIETY OF KEYS. YOU MUST WORK OUT IF THE SCALE IS A NATURAL, HARMONIC OR MELODIC MINOR. REMEMBER TO PAY SPECIAL ATTENTION TO PITCH INTERVALS SURROUND THE SUBMEDIANT AND LEADING NOTES (THE 6TH AND 7TH NOTES). IT IS THESE NOTES THAT PROVIDE THE ANSWERS.

1. ▶ 5 / 7   2. ▶ 5 / 8

3. ▶ 5 / 9   4. ▶ 5 / 10

5. ▶ 5 / 11   6. ▶ 5 / 12

7. ▶ 5 / 13   8. ▶ 5 / 14

TIME OUT: SUMMARY OF LESSON 5

∼∼∼∼

HERE IS A SUMMARY OF THE MAJOR POINTS SHOWN IN THIS LESSON.

- THE NATURAL MINOR SCALE
- RELATIVE MAJORS AND RELATIVE MINORS
- RELATIVE MINOR KEY SIGNATURES
- THE HARMONIC MINOR SCALE

- NAMING THE SCALE DEGREES
- THE MELODIC MINOR SCALE (ASCENDING)
- THE MELODIC MINOR SCALE (DESCENDING)
- DOUBLE SHARPS AND DOUBLE FLATS

LESSON 6:

Intervals

An INTERVAL is the distance between two notes. There are two distinct types of interval: if the two notes are played at the same time it is called a HARMONIC INTERVAL; if they are played separately it is MELODIC INTERVAL. Although some people can be heard referring to a harmonic interval as a type of chord, this is not technically correct – a chord requires three different pitches.

HEARING THE INTERVALS

Look at the three staves shown below. The example at the top illustrates a harmonic interval built from the notes C and a higher-pitched G. The notes are played at the same time. The second example shows an ascending melodic interval using the same two notes. In this case, the lower note (C) is followed by the higher-pitched note (G). The example at the foot of the page illustrates a descending melodic interval in which the higher-pitched note is followed by the lower-pitched note.

NUMBERING THE INTERVALS

As we have already seen in lessons 3 and 5, every scale is made up a fixed set of intervals from the root which remains the same irrespective of the key being used. These intervals can be named by counting from the lowest-pitched note through the degrees of the scale until you reach the highest-pitch note. For example, in the key of C major, the interval between the notes C and D is a known as a SECOND (D is the second degree of the C major scale). Similarly, the interval between C and E is a THIRD, and so on. When they are written down, these intervals are invariably shown numerically – the examples above are would thus become 2ND and 3RD respectively.

NAMING THE INTERVALS

Intervals can be named within any type of scale. Therefore, labelling them by the distance between the notes is not always sufficient. For example, the notes that make up an interval of a 3rd in a C major scale are C and E, but in a C minor scale they are C and E♭. To overcome this problem, a prefix is added to describe the "quality" of the relationship between the notes and to provide the interval with an

HARMONIC   ▶ 6/1

ASCENDING MELODIC   ▶ 6/2

DESCENDING MELODIC   ▶ 6/3

unequivocally unique label. In a major scale, the term "perfect" is used to describe the 4th and 5th degrees of the scale (as well as the octave); the other degrees are prefixed with "major". The interval between C and E♭ is termed a MINOR 3rd.

A full set of interval names are shown below for all of the notes that make up the key of C major. Notice also that the abbreviation for the octave – "8ve" – has been used in the last example. This is commonly used shorthand.   ▶ 6 / 4

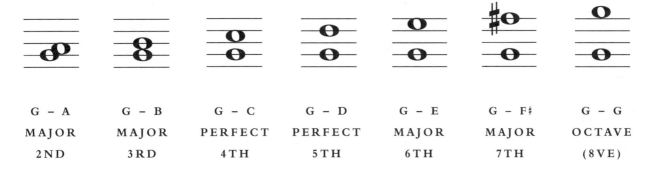

C – D	C – E	C – F	C – G	C – A	C – B	C – C
MAJOR	MAJOR	PERFECT	PERFECT	MAJOR	MAJOR	OCTAVE
2ND	3RD	4TH	5TH	6TH	7TH	(8VE)

TRANSPOSING THE INTERVALS

Although the intervals are shown above in the key of C major, the names and relationships remain the same for ever other key. To illustrate this point, the same set of harmonic intervals is shown below this time in the key of G major. The interval between C and D (above) is identical to the interval between G and A (below). This process is known as TRANSPOSITION. It's possible to transpose a set of notes up or down by a specified interval. This has the effect of changing key. In this example, the notes have been transposed from C major to G major, or up by a perfect 5th. Transposition will be covered in greater depth at the end of this lesson.   ▶ 6 / 5

G – A	G – B	G – C	G – D	G – E	G – F♯	G – G
MAJOR	MAJOR	PERFECT	PERFECT	MAJOR	MAJOR	OCTAVE
2ND	3RD	4TH	5TH	6TH	7TH	(8VE)

MELODIC INTERVALS

On the staff below, the seven intervals that were shown above harmonically in the key C major have been written down as a sequence of melodic intervals. They are marked as seven distinct pairs. Thus, the first two notes – C and D – make up an ascending major 2nd interval. However, if you now look at the second and third notes – D to C – you will see that they create a descending major 2nd interval. This pattern is followed through to the end of the sequence. You can hear the complete sequence on track 6/6 of the CD.   ▶ 6 / 6

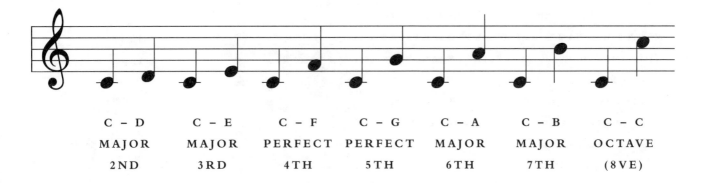

C – D	C – E	C – F	C – G	C – A	C – B	C – C
MAJOR	MAJOR	PERFECT	PERFECT	MAJOR	MAJOR	OCTAVE
2ND	3RD	4TH	5TH	6TH	7TH	(8VE)

AURAL INTERPRETATION OF HARMONIC INTERVALS

When you are not accustomed to hearing two different pitches played at the same time it can be difficult to predict how any two notes will sound together. The reverse is also true, in that when you hear combinations of notes played together it can be challenging for the untutored ear to pick out the individual notes. This becomes even more complex when dealing with chords containing upwards of three different notes. It is therefore useful to be able to make the connection between how the same set of intervals sound when played both melodically and harmonically.

Try the experiment shown below. The first bar contains harmonic intervals, the second melodic intervals. If you play through the sequence a few times you will quickly hear the similarities between the two bars. In time, and with practice, you will be able to hear an type of harmonic interval and almost instinctively be able to name the relationship between the two notes.

 6 / 7

FROM MELODIC TO HARMONIC

The next experiment is effectively the reverse of the one shown above. The first bar contains melodic intervals of a major 3rd; the second bar contains harmonic intervals of the same value. Start off by slowly playing the notes as a repeated sequence. If you proceed to play the two bars at an increasingly fast tempo the two single notes in the first bar will seem to "blur" together, almost creating an illusion of being played at the same time. Of course, no matter how fast the tempo, the single notes will never actually merge together, but once again it provides a way of connecting the two different very distinct types of musical effect.

 6 / 8

INVERTING INTERVALS

∞∞∞∞

IF YOU TAKE AN INTERVAL OF A PERFECT 5TH IN THE KEY OF C, THE TWO NOTES ARE C AND G. IN SUCH A RELATIONSHIP THE G WILL ALWAYS BE HIGHER IN PITCH THAN C. BUT WHAT HAPPENS IF YOU RAISE THE PITCH OF C BY AN OCTAVE? YOU MIGHT THINK THAT BECAUSE THE TWO NOTES ARE THE SAME, THE INTERVAL IS ALSO THE SAME. THIS IS NOT THE CASE. IF YOU LOOK AT THE INTERVAL NAMES FOR G MAJOR ON THE PREVIOUS PAGE YOU WILL SEE THAT AN INTERVAL BETWEEN G AND A HIGHER-PITCHED C IS A PERFECT 4TH. ALTHOUGH THE TWO NOTES STILL MAKE A PLEASANT SOUND WHEN PLAYED TOGETHER, YOU CAN HEAR THAT THE MUSICAL EFFECT CREATED IS NOT THE SAME. THIS PROCESS IS KNOWN AS "INVERSION". IT WILL BE DISCUSSED IN GREATER DEPTH DURING THE NEXT LESSON.

PERFECT 5TH   PERFECT 4TH

(C – G)   (G – C)

 6 / 9

TEST 17

〜〜〜〜

HERE ARE FIVE EXERCISES.
EACH ONE SHOWS EIGHT SETS OF HARMONIC
INTERVALS. YOUR TASK IS TO NAME EACH INTERVAL.
TO MAKE THE TEST MORE DEMANDING A SELECTION
OF DIFFERENT KEYS HAVE BEEN USED.
TO WORK OUT THE ANSWERS YOU FIRST NEED TO
IDENTIFY THE TWO NOTE NAMES. WHEN YOU'VE

DONE THAT, TAKE THE LOWEST-PITCHED NOTE AS
THE ROOT OF THE MAJOR SCALE AND COUNT
THROUGH EACH DEGREE UNTIL YOU REACH THE
HIGHER-PITCHED NOTE. AS THE EXERCISES ARE ALL
MAJOR-SCALE INTERVALS, THE ANSWERS MUST BE
ONE OF THE FOLLOWING: MAJOR 2ND, MAJOR 3RD,
PERFECT 4TH, PERFECT 5TH, MAJOR 6TH, MAJOR 7TH
OR 8VE. TO MAKE THE TEST MORE OF A CHALLENGE,
EXERCISES 33-40 USE NOTES ON THE BASS CLEF.

(33-40 ON THE BASS CLEF)

MINOR-SCALE INTERVALS

The 1st, 2nd, 4th, 5th and 8th degrees remain the same for all of the diatonic scales. However, among the minor keys, the 3rd degree is always flattened and the 6th and 7th degrees alter depending on the type of minor scale being used and, when using the melodic minor, whether you are ascending or descending the scale. So for naming minor-scale intervals, three new labels are required. The flattened 3rd, 6th and 7th degrees become MINOR 3RD, MINOR 6TH and MINOR 7TH intervals respectively.

The complete set of diatonic intervals are shown on the staff below. Furthermore, a list of the intervals for each degree of all four diatonic scales are shown on the right. ▷ 6 / 10

INTERVAL SET
∞∞∞∞

MAJOR	NATURAL MINOR	HARMONIC MINOR	MELODIC MINOR (ASCENDING)
UNISON	UNISON	UNISON	UNISON
MAJ 2ND	MAJ 2ND	MAJ 2ND	MAJ 2ND
MAJ 3RD	MIN 3RD	MIN 3RD	MIN 3RD
PERF 4TH	PERF 4TH	PERF 4TH	PERF 4TH
PERF 5TH	PERF 5TH	PERF 5TH	PERF 5TH
MAJ 6TH	MIN 6TH	MIN 6TH	MAJ 6TH
MAJ 7TH	MIN 7TH	MAJ 7TH	MAJ 7TH
8VE	8VE	8VE	8VE

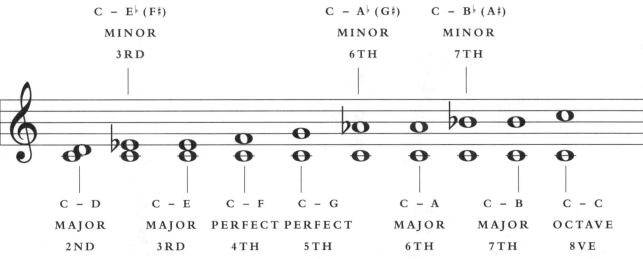

C – E♭ (F♯) MINOR 3RD   C – A♭ (G♯) MINOR 6TH   C – B♭ (A♯) MINOR 7TH

C – D MAJOR 2ND   C – E MAJOR 3RD   C – F PERFECT 4TH   C – G PERFECT 5TH   C – A MAJOR 6TH   C – B MAJOR 7TH   C – C OCTAVE 8VE

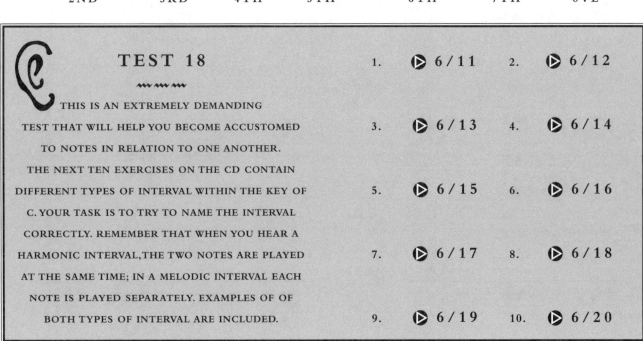

TEST 18
∿∿∿∿

THIS IS AN EXTREMELY DEMANDING TEST THAT WILL HELP YOU BECOME ACCUSTOMED TO NOTES IN RELATION TO ONE ANOTHER. THE NEXT TEN EXERCISES ON THE CD CONTAIN DIFFERENT TYPES OF INTERVAL WITHIN THE KEY OF C. YOUR TASK IS TO TRY TO NAME THE INTERVAL CORRECTLY. REMEMBER THAT WHEN YOU HEAR A HARMONIC INTERVAL, THE TWO NOTES ARE PLAYED AT THE SAME TIME; IN A MELODIC INTERVAL EACH NOTE IS PLAYED SEPARATELY. EXAMPLES OF OF BOTH TYPES OF INTERVAL ARE INCLUDED.

1. ▷ 6 / 11   2. ▷ 6 / 12

3. ▷ 6 / 13   4. ▷ 6 / 14

5. ▷ 6 / 15   6. ▷ 6 / 16

7. ▷ 6 / 17   8. ▷ 6 / 18

9. ▷ 6 / 19   10. ▷ 6 / 20

CHROMATIC INTERVALS

All intervals that are not diatonic – those that are not part of the major or minor scales – are termed CHROMATIC. You may have noticed that there are two possible intervals not listed on the staff across the page. These intervals – C to D♭ and C to F♯ – are chromatic because they do not appear in the major or minor scales for the key of C.

Take a look at the first of those chromatic intervals – C to D♭. This can be named as a MINOR 2ND. It does, however, raise a further question: if the upper note used its enharmonic equivalent, becoming C♯, would the interval still be a minor 2nd? In fact, in spite of the two notes being identical in pitch, the interval would take on a new name. Since C♯ is C raised by a semitone, we need a new description to take account of the altered enharmonic names. Thus, the prefix AUGMENTED is used. Rather than calling the interval between C and C when the pitch is identical a 1st, as would be logically consistent with the other labels, it is instead called a UNISON. Thus, although the the intervals between C and D♭, and C and C♯ sound identical, they take two different names depending on their use: C to D♭ is a MINOR 2ND; C to C♯ is a UNISON AUGMENTED. In fact, the interval between C and C♯ is known as a "chromatic semitone" because it is not used in any diatonic scale; C to D♭, on the other hand, whilst a chromatic interval in the context of the key of C major, *does* appear in other diatonic keys (A♭ major and F natural and harmonic minors, for example). It is thus known as a "diatonic semitone".

The opposite effect of an augmented note is one that is DIMINISHED, which flattens the the upper note, lowering it in pitch by a semitone.

THE FULL SET

We now have the full set of "qualities" used to describe intervals between any two degrees of any type of scale. They are: perfect, major, minor, augmented and diminished.

Intervals with a value of a 2nd, 3rd, 6th and 7th can be diminished, minor, major or augmented; intervals of a unison, 4th, 5th and 8ve can only be diminished, perfect or augmented.

SHORTHAND NOTATION FOR INTERVALS

∞∞∞∞

FOR CONVENIENCE, INTERVALS CAN BE NOTATED IN SHORTHAND USING A VARIETY OF DIFFERENT SYMBOLS.

A MAJOR OR PERFECT INTERVAL CAN BE SHOWN AS UPPER-CASE ROMAN NUMERALS. FOR EXAMPLE, A MAJOR 7TH CAN BE NOTATED AS "VII".

MINOR EQUIVALENTS ARE SHOWN IN LOWER-CASE ROMAN NUMERALS, THUS A MINOR 7TH CAN BE NOTATED AS "vii".

AUGMENTED INTERVALS ARE INDICATED WITH A "PLUS" SIGN AND DIMINISHED INTERVALS WITH A "DEGREE" SYMBOL. THUS, "V+" SIGNIFIES AN AUGMENTED 5TH AND "V°" DENOTES A DIMINISHED 5TH.

I - UNISON
II° – DIMINISHED 2ND
ii - MINOR 2ND
II - MAJOR 2ND
iii - MINOR 3RD
III° - DIMINISHED 3RD
III - MAJOR 3RD
III+ - AUGMENTED 3RD
IV° - DIMINISHED 4TH
IV - PERFECT 4TH
IV+ - AUGMENTED 4TH
V° - DIMINISHED 5TH
V - PERFECT 5TH
V+ AUGMENTED 5TH
vi - MINOR 6TH
VI° - DIMINISHED 6TH
VI - MAJOR 6TH
VI+ AUGMENTED 6TH
VII - DIMINISHED 7TH
vii – MINOR 7TH
VII - MAJOR 7TH
VII+ AUGMENTED 7TH
VIII (8VE) - OCTAVE

THE FULL RANGE OF INTERVALS

A full range of interval names for the key of C is shown in this table below. Enharmonic equivalents are linked by a line – the augmented 4th between C and F# has the same pitch value as the diminished 5th between C and G♭. Notice also that the double-flat symbol (♭♭) is used here. In the case of the minor 2nd, because the higher note of this interval has already been flattened, diminishing the note adds a further flat. In fact, D♭♭ has the same pitch as C.

There *are* other possible intervals within a single octave. These require the introduction of such terms as "doubly-augmented" and "doubly-diminished". Their use is very rare.

We can summarize the way in which interval names work in these four simple rules:

• Raising a major or perfect interval by a semitone, will create an AUGMENTED interval.

• Raising a minor interval by a semitone, creates a MAJOR interval.

• Lowering a perfect or minor interval by a semitone, creates an DIMINISHED interval.

• Lowering a major interval by a semitone, creates a MINOR interval.

C – C♭	C – C	C – C#	C – D♭♭	C – D♭
DIMINISHED UNISON	PERFECT UNISON	AUGMENTED UNISON	DIMINISHED 2ND	MINOR 2ND

C – D	C – D#	C – E♭♭	C – E♭
MAJOR 2ND	AUGMENTED 2ND	DIMINISHED 3RD	MINOR 3RD

C – E	C – E#	C – F♭	C – F	C – F#	C – G♭
MAJOR 3RD	AUGMENTED 3RD	DIMINISHED 4TH	PERFECT 4TH	AUGMENTED 4TH	DIMINISHED 5TH

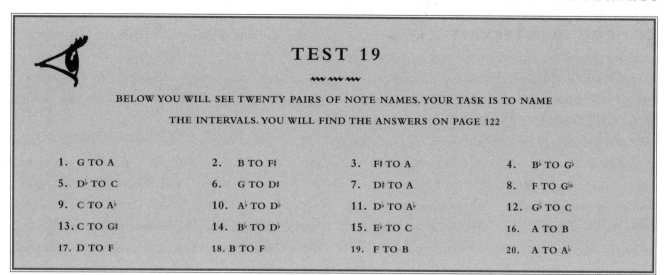

TEST 19

BELOW YOU WILL SEE TWENTY PAIRS OF NOTE NAMES. YOUR TASK IS TO NAME

THE INTERVALS. YOU WILL FIND THE ANSWERS ON PAGE 122

1. G TO A
2. B TO F♯
3. F♯ TO A
4. B♭ TO G♭
5. D♭ TO C
6. G TO D♯
7. D♯ TO A
8. F TO G♭♭
9. C TO A♭
10. A♭ TO D♭
11. D♭ TO A♭
12. G♭ TO C
13. C TO G♯
14. B♭ TO D♭
15. E♭ TO C
16. A TO B
17. D TO F
18. B TO F
19. F TO B
20. A TO A♭

COMPOUND INTERVALS

So far throughout this lesson we have been looking at intervals within a single octave. It is also possible to extend intervals beyond the octave. These are known as COMPOUND INTERVALS. Naming standards for these intervals follow exactly the same principles as within the octave except that you count beyond eight – the octave number. This can be slightly confusing as you might imagine that the interval numbers beyond the octave take on the original intervalic value plus eight – the number of notes in the octave. This is not the case because the octave takes the same note name as the unison. Thus, if you count past the octave, the first degree you reach is the 9th, which in the key of C is the note D – this is the same note as the 2nd. If you continue counting upwards you will reach the 15th, the same note as both the root and the octave.

Compound intervals use identical prefixes. Thus, just as the an interval between C and E is a major 3rd, the interval between C and E beyond the octave is a major 10th. The staff below shows two octaves of compound intervals. An understanding of the way intervals work is a vital part of many practical aspects of music, such as understanding how chords are constructed.

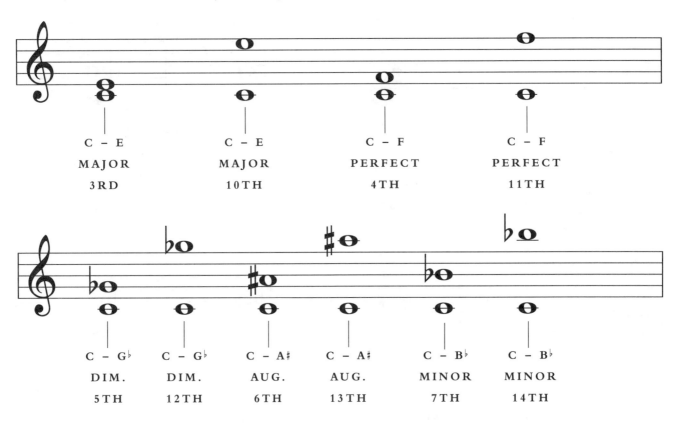

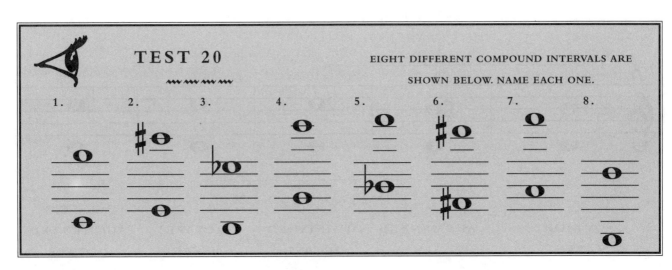

TRANSPOSITION

The term TRANSPOSITION refers to a set of notes being moved up or down in pitch. For this to be correct, ALL of the notes in the piece of music must be moved by the same value – that is, the intervals by which they are moved always remain the same. In fact you have already come across one example of transposition earlier in this lesson when the harmonic intervals for C major were then shown for G major. In the this instance, the sequence of notes were transposes up by a perfect 5th. Any sequence of notes can be moved up or down by any interval.

Look at the first two examples shown below. The first staff is a simple tune in the key of C. Directly below you will see the same piece of music transposed UP by a major 3rd. Compare each of the individual notes in each sequence. You will see that in all cases there is an interval of a major 3rd between both sets of notes.

Similarly – or consequently, in fact – the melodic intervals between each of the notes in the sequence also remains the same. If you look at the first two notes of the first sequence you'll see that the interval between C and E is a major 3rd. Now look at the first two notes of the second sequence – the interval between E and G♯ is a also a major 3rd.

You can hear the two pieces played one after the other on the CD.   ▶ 6 / 21

TRANSPOSING DOWN

It is also possible to transpose the pitch of a piece of music downward. This example is the same as the piece above only it has been transposed DOWN by an interval of a minor 3rd. Thus, the first note of sequence descends from C down to A. Again, if you check the melodic interval between the first two notes – A to C♯ – it remains a major 3rd.

The facility to transpose music has a multitude of uses. It can used to "tune" a piece of music to the range of the singer's voice. If you are arranging ensemble music, you need to be aware that there are some instruments, such as the trumpet, that automatically transpose – when a trumpeter plays a note written as C, the pitch of sound you hear will be B♭ (see page 100).   ▶ 6 / 22

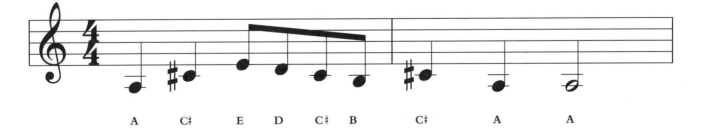

CHANGING KEYS

If an entire piece of music is transposed, then the key is automatically changed. By moving a piece of music written in C major UP by a major 3rd – as in the example on the previous page – the key is changed from C major to E major. Similarly, by transposing the original sequence down by a minor 3rd, the key changes from C to A major. In those examples, the resulting transpositions were written out in full to show the effect clearly. To be technically correct, the new notation should have taken into account the two new keys – the key signatures should have been shown at the beginning of the staff.

As you can see from the revised staves below, when the key signatures are shown at the beginning of the staves, the accidentals – in these examples, sharps – no longer have to shown throughout the score. The first example is now correctly shown in the key of E major, with its "four sharps" at the start of the line. The sharp symbols alongside the notes G and F are no longer needed – the key signature tells the player that unless otherwise shown, the notes C, D, F and G are sharps. The second example is also correctly shown in the key of "three sharps" – A major.

If you're still uncertain about how key signatures work, take another look at the end of lesson 4.

CONSONANCE AND DISSONANCE

∞∞∞∞

AS YOU HAVE BEEN WORKING THROUGH THIS LESSON, YOU WILL NO DOUBT HAVE BECOME AWARE OF THE FACT THAT SOME OF THESE HARMONIC INTERVALS SEEM TO "WORK" BETTER THAN OTHERS. THE MUSICAL TERMS TO DESCRIBE THIS KIND OF EFFECT ARE CONCORD AND DISCORD. ALTHOUGH THESE WORDS ARE SOMETIMES USED VERY LOOSELY TO DESCRIBE WHETHER A PIECE OF MUSIC IS PLEASING TO THE EARS, THEY HAVE VERY SPECIFIC MUSICAL MEANINGS.

ALL INTERVALS CAN BE DESCRIBED IN TERMS OF BEING EITHER CONSONANT OR DISSONANT. THERE ARE TWO DISTINCT CATEGORIES OF

CONSONANCE. PERFECT CONCORDS ARE THE "PERFECT" INTERVALS: UNISON, PERFECT 4TH, PERFECT 5TH AND OCTAVE. THE IMPERFECT CONCORDS ARE THE MINOR 3RD AND MINOR 6TH INTERVALS. ALL OTHER INTERVALS, INCLUDING THOSE THAT ARE AUGMENTED OR DIMINISHED, ARE DEEMED TO BE DISSONANT.

CONCORDS AND DISCORDS ARE OFTEN DISCUSSED IN TERMS OF THEIR MUSICAL "STABILITY". DISSONANT INTERVALS ARE DEEMED TO BE UNSTABLE IN THEIR OWN RIGHT, SEEMINGLY REQUIRING THAT ONE THE TWO NOTES BE MOVED A SEMITONE UP OR DOWN TO "RESOLVE" ITSELF. THIS ISSUE IS SLIGHTLY COMPLICATED BY THE PERFECT 4TH WHICH ALTHOUGH A PERFECT CONCORD CAN, IN SOME CONTEXTS, BE DISSONANT.

TEST 21

BELOW YOU WILL SEE TEN SINGLE BARS OF MUSIC. IN EACH CASE YOU WILL BE ASKED TO TRANSPOSE THE NOTES EITHER BY A SPECIFIC INTERVAL OR INTO ANOTHER KEY (THE INSTRUCTION APPEARS ALONGSIDE THE EXERCISE NUMBER). REMEMBER THAT AS YOU ARE CHANGING KEYS YOU WILL NEED TO GIVE THE RESULTING TRANSPOSITIONS NEW KEY SIGNATURES.

1. UP MAJOR 3RD

2. DOWN MINOR 7TH

3. C MAJOR

4. UP PERFECT 4TH

5. DOWN PERFECT 5TH

6. DOWN MAJOR 3RD

7. A MAJOR

8. UP MINOR 2ND

9. UP PERFECT 5TH

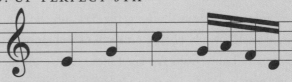

10. DOWN MINOR 2ND

TIME OUT: SUMMARY OF LESSON 6

HERE IS A SUMMARY OF THE MAJOR POINTS SHOWN IN THIS LESSON. IF YOU ARE UNCERTAIN OF ANY OF THE SUBJECTS LIST REVIEW THEM BEFORE YOU MOVE ONTO LESSON 7.

- HARMONIC INTERVALS
- MELODIC INTERVALS
- NAMING DIATONIC INTERVALS
- INVERTING INTERVALS
- NAMING CHROMATIC INTERVALS

- COMPOUND INTERVALS
- TRANSPOSITION
- CHANGING KEY SIGNATURES
- CONCORD
- DISCORD

LESSON 7:

Harmonic Theory

Music is often informally broken into three components: rhythm, melody and harmony. An important distinction needs to be made between the latter two elements. Melody refers to the deliberate arrangement of series of pitches — what most people would call a tune. Harmony, on the other hand, deals with pitches that are played at the same time. When three or more different notes sound together the resulting effect is a CHORD.

TRIADS

The simplest form of chord is called a TRIAD. The name triad is derived from the fact that this type of a chord comprises three notes. Triads are built from a root note and follow a specific set of intervals. The three notes are always the root, the 3rd and the 5th. This, in itself, already poses a problem of ambiguity: as you already know from the last lesson, such numeric descriptions are not unique in identifying an interval. Thus we also must consider what type of 3rd and 5th interval to use.

There are four different kinds of triad, each of which uses 3rds and 5ths of differing "qualities". The MAJOR TRIAD consists of the root, major 3rd and perfect 5th. In the key of C, as shown on the right, the notes C, E and G are used. This combination of notes is commonly referred to as C MAJOR.

The MINOR TRIAD consists of the root, minor 3rd and perfect 5th. In the key of C it uses the notes C, E♭ and G. This chord is often known simply as C MINOR.

The DIMINISHED TRIAD is made up from the root, minor 3rd and diminished 5th intervals. In the key of C the notes used are C, E♭ and G♭.

Finally, the AUGMENTED TRIAD comprises the root, major 3rd and augmented 5th intervals. In the key of C the notes required are C, E and G♯.

C MAJOR TRIAD

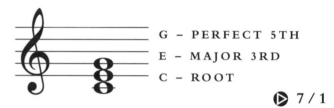

G – PERFECT 5TH
E – MAJOR 3RD
C – ROOT

▶ 7 / 1

C MINOR TRIAD

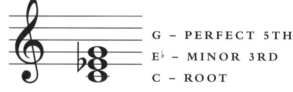

G – PERFECT 5TH
E♭ – MINOR 3RD
C – ROOT

▶ 7 / 2

C DIMINISHED TRIAD

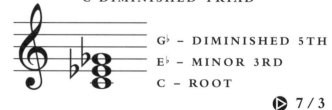

G♭ – DIMINISHED 5TH
E♭ – MINOR 3RD
C – ROOT

▶ 7 / 3

C AUGMENTED TRIAD

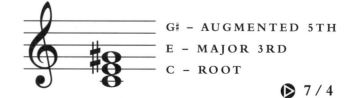

G♯ – AUGMENTED 5TH
E – MAJOR 3RD
C – ROOT

▶ 7 / 4

TRIADS ON THE MAJOR SCALE

The most fundamentally important aspect of harmonic theory is the way in which chordal effects sound when played alongside one another – indeed, it is at the very heart of most Western musical forms. As you already know how the notes of a diatonic scale relate to each other, the most effective way of showing these chord relationships is by building a series of triads from a diatonic major scale.

The staff below shows what amounts to a scale of chords. But although it is a major scale, you will see that it is not only made up from major triads. In fact, minor and diminished triads are also used.

Play through this sequence or listen to it on the CD. Listen to the smooth manner in which the triads flow into one another, and notice how satisfactorily the 7th degree (B diminished) resolves back to C major. ▶ 7 / 5

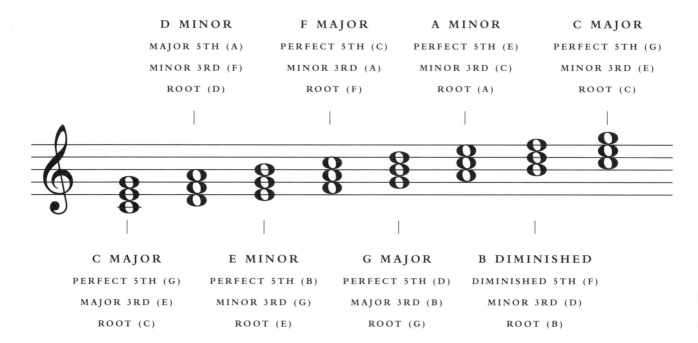

D MINOR	F MAJOR	A MINOR	C MAJOR
MAJOR 5TH (A)	PERFECT 5TH (C)	PERFECT 5TH (E)	PERFECT 5TH (G)
MINOR 3RD (F)	MINOR 3RD (A)	MINOR 3RD (C)	MINOR 3RD (E)
ROOT (D)	ROOT (F)	ROOT (A)	ROOT (C)

C MAJOR	E MINOR	G MAJOR	B DIMINISHED
PERFECT 5TH (G)	PERFECT 5TH (B)	PERFECT 5TH (D)	DIMINISHED 5TH (F)
MAJOR 3RD (E)	MINOR 3RD (G)	MAJOR 3RD (B)	MINOR 3RD (D)
ROOT (C)	ROOT (E)	ROOT (G)	ROOT (B)

THE SPECIAL RELATIONSHIP

The triads on the major scale can also be named after the degrees on on which they are constructed. In the example above, C major on the 1st degree can be called the TONIC TRIAD. Similarly, D minor on the 2nd degree may be called the SUPERTONIC triad and so forth (you can refer back to page 52 if you need a reminder of the other names).

The degrees themselves can also be used as a kind of shorthand description. Thus, in the key of key of C, a "V" chord is G major – the DOMINANT TRIAD – because it is built from the 5th degree. This approach is

sometimes used within informal musical settings where a "one-four-five in G" would mean a chord sequence revolving around the chord progression G major ("I"), C major ("IV") and D major ("V").

You may have already gleaned from previous lessons that there is a very special musical relationship between the 1st, 4th and 5th degrees – they are not called the "perfect intervals" for no reason. The importance of this relationship will gradually become even clearer as your understanding of harmony grows. In fact, the "I", "IV" and "V" triads are also termed the PRIMARY TRIADS. ▶ 7 / 6

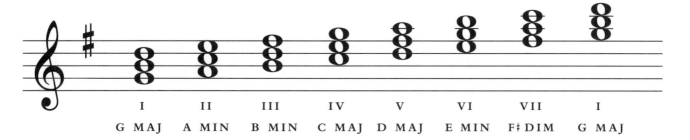

I	II	III	IV	V	VI	VII	I
G MAJ	A MIN	B MIN	C MAJ	D MAJ	E MIN	F♯ DIM	G MAJ

MINOR TRIADS

Triads can also be built from each degree of the minor scale. However matters here are less clear-cut because of the differences between the natural, melodic and harmonic minor scales. Therefore the triads themselves can be varied. Indeed, with the exception of the tonic triad there is an alternative for every other degree.

A full set is shown below for the key of C minor. It can also be heard on track 7/7 of the CD. The scale shows a full complement of major, minor, diminished and augmented triads.

▶ 7 / 7

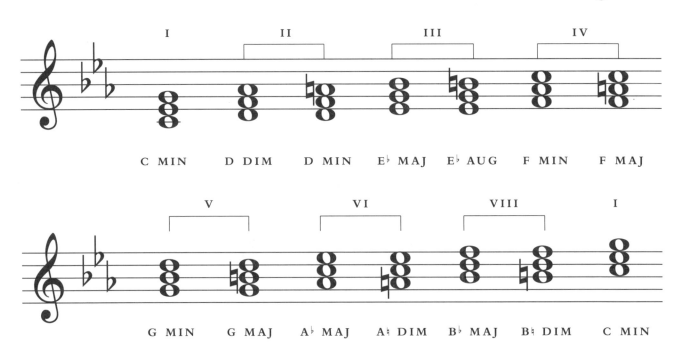

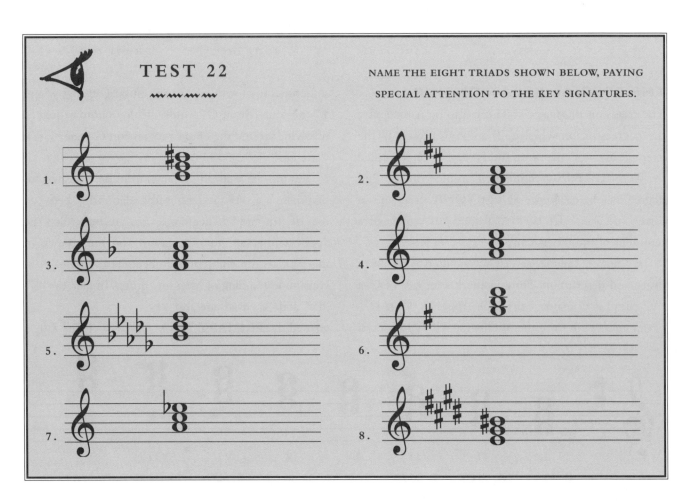

BREAKING UP THE TRIADS

To help you get used to the distinctive sounds made by the four different types of triad you first need to acquaint yourself with the sound of the intervals between the notes that create the triads. This next set of exercises is a slightly more advanced variation on the aural interpretation exercises from lesson 6.

Each of the four staves below contains a different kind of triad in C. The first bar deconstructs the triad into a set of melodic intervals; the second bar plays the notes in their triadic form.

If you repeat each sequence a few times you will quickly be able to connect the sound made by the melodic intervals with the sound of the three notes played at the same time. Equally, treating the four examples as a single sequence of eight bars will fix the contrasts between each triad in your mind – they are presented this way on the CD.

For ease of comparison, the four triads have been shown in C major. In practice both the minor and diminished triads would more likely take a key signature of C minor.   ▶ 7 / 8

MAJOR

MINOR

DIMINISHED

AUGMENTED

TEST 23

LISTEN TO THE NEXT SIX TRACKS
ON THE CD. EACH ONE IS A TRIAD. YOUR TASK IS
SIMPLY TO NAME THE TYPE OF THE TRIAD BEING
PLAYED. TO MAKE THIS MORE DIFFICULT THEY ARE
PLAYED IN A NUMBER OF DIFFERENT KEYS.

1. ▶ 7 / 9   2. ▶ 7 / 10

3. ▶ 7 / 11   4. ▶ 7 / 12

5. ▶ 7 / 13   6. ▶ 7 / 14

INVERSION

The triads you seen so far have all been played according to a strict sequence where the root, 3rd and 5th notes have all been successively higher in pitch. This need not always be the case. What, for example, if a C major triad was constructed with the root note – C – ABOVE the 3rd and the 5th? As the lowest note is now E, does it shift to the key of E? The answer is that it remains a C major triad. If, however, you listen to the two triads played together you will notice that they clearly have different emphasis in their sound. If you like, they sound the same and yet somehow "different".

The term INVERSION is used to describe triads that change in this way. A triad whose 3rd is the lowest in pitch is called a FIRST INVERSION. That same triad can be further rearranged so that the 5th is the lowest in pitch. This is known as a SECOND INVERSION.

You can hear the way the triad sounds alongside its two inversions on track 7/15 of the CD. They are shown on the staves below. ▶ **7 / 15**

C MAJOR TRIAD   C MAJOR TRIAD   C MAJOR TRIAD
(ROOT POSITION)   (FIRST INVERSION)   (SECOND INVERSION)

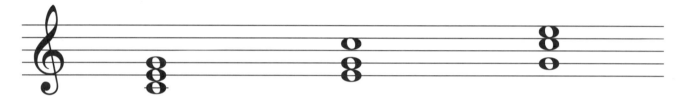

G – PERFECT 5TH   C – ROOT   E – MAJOR 3RD
E – MAJOR 3RD   G – PERFECT 5TH   C – ROOT
C – ROOT   E – MAJOR 3RD   G – PERFECT 5TH

INVERSION AND INTERVALS

A slightly confusing issue for beginners when dealing with inversions of triads is that of the new intervals created. We know that a basic C major triad is built from the root (C), major 3rd (E) and perfect 5th (G), with the notes appearing in order of ascending pitch. However, in its first inversion, C major then becomes Major 3rd (E), major 5th (G) and root (C) meaning that the intervals between the two highest-pitched notes have changed from a 3rd (E to G) to a 4th (G to C). Does this, therefore, mean that the intervals that define a triad are not always consistent? No, the answer is simply that when we refer to the 3rds and 5ths within any of the four triadic forms, we are ALWAYS referring to the intervals as they were in the root position.

NAMING INVERSIONS
∞∞∞∞

THE ABBREVIATED NAMES GIVEN TO THE TRIADS FORMED ON THE SCALE CAN BE FURTHER EXTENDED TO COVER INVERSIONS. THE ROMAN NUMERALS CAN BE SUFFIXED WITH A LOWER-CASE "a" TO INDICATE A ROOT POSITION; "b" TO INDICATE A FIRST INVERSION; AND "c" TO INDICATE A SECOND INVERSION. IN THIS WAY, "IIa" IS THE ROOT POSITION OF THE SUPERTONIC TRIAD, "IVb" THE FIRST INVERSION OF THE SUBDOMINANT TRIAD, AND "VIIc" IS THE SECOND INVERSION OF THE LEADING NOTE TRIAD. FOR THE KEY OF C THESE TRIADS ARE D MINOR, F MAJOR AND B DIMINISHED RESPECTIVELY.

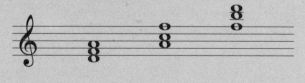

IIa   IVb   VIIc

OPEN POSITION TRIADS

Irrespective of which type of inversion has been used, each of the triads you have seen so far can be referred to as being in the CLOSE POSITION. This describes a triad where all of the notes are grouped as closely as possible to one another. Triads can also be grouped in the OPEN POSITION. This is where the notes are spaced out so that there is an interval of more than an octave between the highest and lowest notes.

If we take a root position G major triad and raise the 3rd (B) by an octave, although it changes the character of the triad it is NOT in itself an inversion. Because the root remains the lowest pitched note, it is a root triad in the open position.

Triads with first and second inversions can be created in the open position. In the second example in G major, the 5th (D) has been raised by an octave, and in the third example the root (G) has also been raised by the octave. ▶ 7 / 16

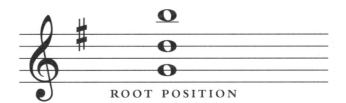

ROOT POSITION

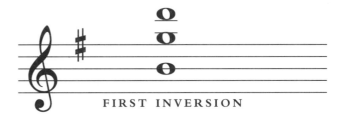

FIRST INVERSION

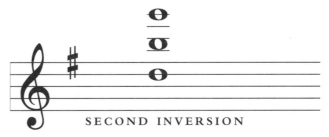

SECOND INVERSION

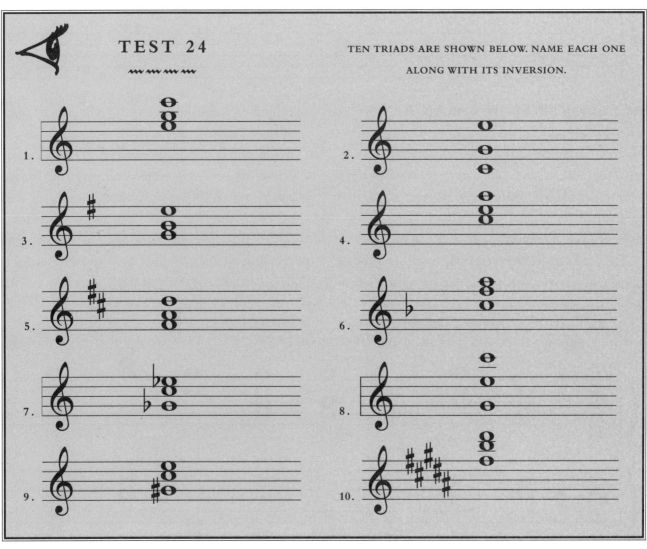

TEST 24

TEN TRIADS ARE SHOWN BELOW. NAME EACH ONE ALONG WITH ITS INVERSION.

WHAT IS A CHORD?

A triad is the simplest type of chord. But irrespective of its arrangement, as long as it comprizes just three differently pitched notes it will always remain a triad.

Although you have seen how different musical effects can be created by using the two alternative inversions or using the open position, it still gives us a relatively limited palette from which to work. Listen to almost any kind of Western music from any genre – even the simplest pop music – and you will be aware of far more complex harmonic activity. This is achieved in two distinct ways: by the addition of repeated notes from the triad in a different register – intervals of one or more octaves – or the addition of one or more notes that are NOT a part of the original triad.

Perhaps the simplest development between a triad and chord is the addition of a root note one octave below the tonic of triad. In the popular ensemble music of the past 50 years this can be thought of in terms of the role of the bass instrument – usually a bass guitar, double bass, synthesiser or digital sample.

The example below shows how such a bass note can be added to the triads on the C major scale. Listen to the effect it has on the overall sound. Because the notes used are the same, the chord retains its triadic character but has a far greater depth of sound.   ▶ 7 / 17

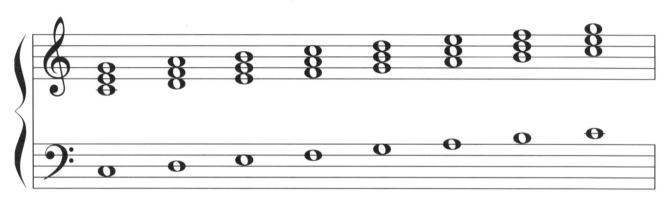

ALTERNATIVES IN C MAJOR

The first element in the staff shown above was the chord C major, consisting of a root position C major triad and the note C an octave below the tonic (shown on the bass staff). There are numerous other possibilities for playing such a chord. These alternatives are known as VOICINGS.

The contrasts can best be heard on a piano or other polyphonic instruments such as the the guitar, where more than one note can be played at the same time.

Monophonic instruments such as brass or reed require an ensemble of musicians to create chords.

A selection of alternative voicings for the G major chord are shown below, scored over two staves for the piano. A variety of different inversions have been used. Note that the final chord in the sequence is made up from eight notes. Such a chord is only possible on a piano or other keyboard instrument – the right hand plays the four treble notes; the left hand plays the four bass notes.   ▶ 7 / 18

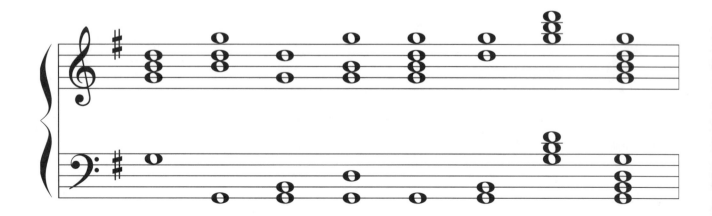

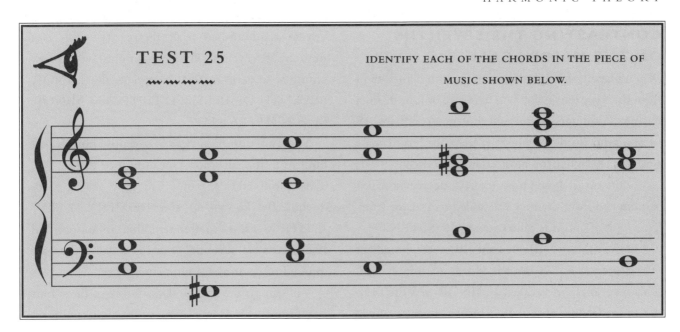

SEVENTH CHORDS

Although repeating the notes of the triad in different ways provides a number of interesting variations, it is by adding notes from outside of the triad that we can create a greater range of harmonic textures. The note most commonly added is 7th – the leading note. This creates a SEVENTH CHORD.

As you know, however, the term "7th note" does not in itself describe a strict pitch within a key. In C, for example, the minor 7th is B♭, the major 7th is B,

the diminished 7th is B♭♭ (the same pitch as A) and the augmented 7th is B♯ (the same pitch as C). Thus, depending on context, it is possible to produce a number of different types of 7th chord. The theory and contrasts can best be seen and heard by adding the 7th to the triads on the C major scale. Each can be named according to its position and abbreviated by its Roman numeral followed by a small seven. Hence, the seventh on the first degree is the TONIC SEVENTH or I⁷.

▶ 7 / 19

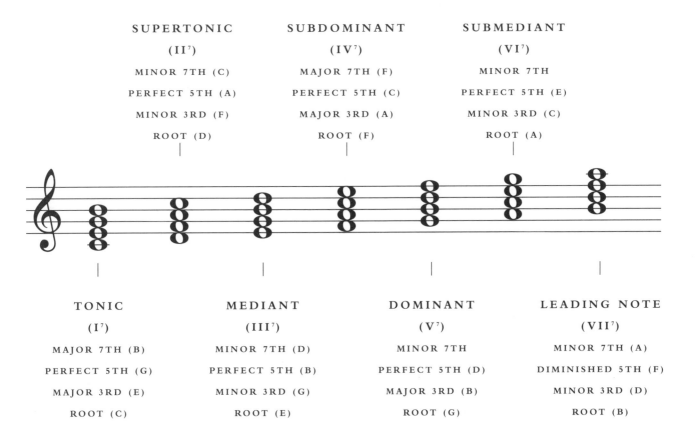

SUPERTONIC (II⁷)	SUBDOMINANT (IV⁷)	SUBMEDIANT (VI⁷)
MINOR 7TH (C)	MAJOR 7TH (F)	MINOR 7TH
PERFECT 5TH (A)	PERFECT 5TH (C)	PERFECT 5TH (E)
MINOR 3RD (F)	MAJOR 3RD (A)	MINOR 3RD (C)
ROOT (D)	ROOT (F)	ROOT (A)

TONIC (I⁷)	MEDIANT (III⁷)	DOMINANT (V⁷)	LEADING NOTE (VII⁷)
MAJOR 7TH (B)	MINOR 7TH (D)	MINOR 7TH	MINOR 7TH (A)
PERFECT 5TH (G)	PERFECT 5TH (B)	PERFECT 5TH (D)	DIMINISHED 5TH (F)
MAJOR 3RD (E)	MINOR 3RD (G)	MAJOR 3RD (B)	MINOR 3RD (D)
ROOT (C)	ROOT (E)	ROOT (G)	ROOT (B)

CONTRASTING THE SEVENTHS ON THE MAJOR SCALE

When playing through the set of seventh chords built from the major scale you will be aware of four distinct flavours. Although, as you will shortly see, other types of seventh chord are possible, the four major-scale sevenths are by far the most commonly used.

On the tonic (I) and subtonic (IV) degrees, a major 7th interval from the root was added to a major triad. This type of chord is called a MAJOR SEVENTH.

On the subtonic (II), mediant (III) and submediant (VI) degrees, a minor 7th was added to a minor triad. This type of chord is called a MINOR SEVENTH.

On the leading note (VII), a minor 7th interval was added to a diminished triad, making a HALF-DIMINISHED SEVENTH. This chord is so named because the triad is diminished but the seventh is not. As you will shortly see, a chord that adds a diminished

7th to a diminished triad also exists – this is a diminished seventh. The half-diminished seventh chord is sometimes also known as the MINOR SEVENTH DIMINISHED FIFTH or a MINOR SEVENTH FLAT FIVE.

The most common type of seventh chord is that built from that all-important dominant degree (V). This chord adds a minor 7th to a major triad. Technically known as the DOMINANT SEVENTH, its use is so frequent that an unspecified reference to a "seventh" chord is usually taken for granted to mean the dominant seventh.

You can get a better understanding of these four contrasting sounds by playing or listening to this set of seventh chords all played with the same root note. Notice from the descriptions that they are NOT, however, in the same key.

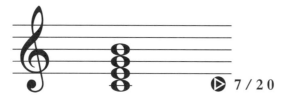

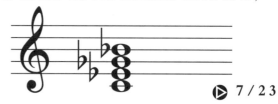

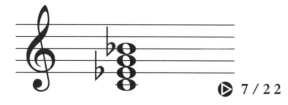

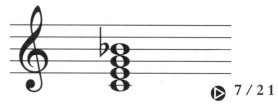

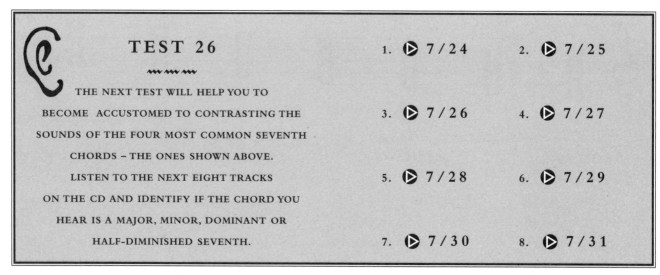

INVERTING CHORDS

∞∼∞∼

THE INVERSION NAMES GIVEN TO MAJOR AND MINOR CHORDS ARE IDENTICAL TO THEIR TRIADIC EQUIVALENT: IF THE ROOT IS THE LOWEST NOTE THEN IT IS A ROOT POSITION ("a"); IF THE 3RD IS THE LOWEST NOTE THEN IT IS A FIRST INVERSION ("b"); AND IF THE 5TH IS THE LOWEST NOTE THEN IT IS A SECOND INVERSION ("c"). THE ISSUE BECOMES MORE COMPLEX WHEN A NOTE FROM OUTSIDE OF THE TRIAD IS INTRODUCED. IN THE CASE OF THE SEVENTH CHORDS, IF THE 7TH IS THE LOWEST NOTE, THEN THE CHORD IS SAID TO BE IN ITS THIRD INVERSION. THIS CAN BE MARKED WITH A LOWER-CASE "d". THE EXAMPLE BELOW SHOWS THE FOUR INVERSIONS OF A C DOMINANT SEVENTH CHORD.

| C7 | C7 | C7 | C7 |
| ROOT (a) | FIRST (b) | SECOND (c) | THIRD (d) |

SEVENTHS ON THE MINOR SCALES

If we add the 7th note to the triads built on natural minor scale, the same set of seventh chords will be produced as in the major scale. Remember that the natural minor scale is also known as the relative minor scale, and furthermore that there is relative minor chord for every major chord (see page 51). Since A minor is the relative minor key of C major, then the seventh chords built on the A natural minor scale will be the same as those used by C major, although in their relative positions. Thus, the sequence for A natural minor is A minor 7th (I), B half-diminished 7th (II), C major 7th (III), D minor 7 (IV), E minor 7 (V), F major 7 (VI) and G 7th (VII).

However, three alternative seventh chords can be created by adding 7th notes to the triads built from the harmonic minor scale. These sevenths, built from the I, III and VII degrees, are less commonly used than those shown across the page. Their practical use may be fairly limited – indeed if they are not used carefully they can sound strange or even simply "wrong".

The MINOR/MAJOR SEVENTH which is shown on the tonic (I) adds a major 7th interval to a minor triad.

The MAJOR SEVENTH AUGMENTED FIFTH appears on the mediant (III) and is an augmented triad with an added major 7th. Technically, the interval added is an augmented major 7th, but it is labelled for simplicity. It is sometimes informally called a "major seven sharp five".

The DIMINISHED SEVENTH is built from the leading note (VII) and adds a diminished 7th to a diminished triad.

You can hear how these new seventh chords sound by playing the complete natural minor sequence shown below.

▶ 7 / 32

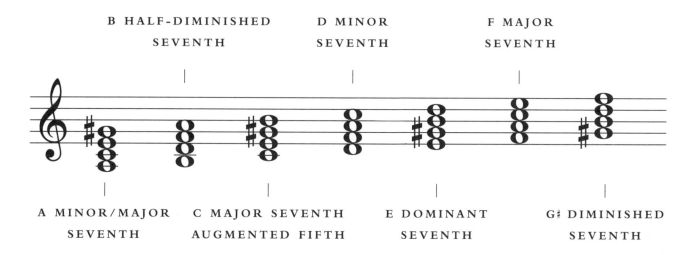

| | B HALF-DIMINISHED SEVENTH | | D MINOR SEVENTH | | F MAJOR SEVENTH |
| A MINOR/MAJOR SEVENTH | C MAJOR SEVENTH AUGMENTED FIFTH | | E DOMINANT SEVENTH | | G♯ DIMINISHED SEVENTH |

ADDING THE SIXTH

So far we have seen how the 1st, 3rd, 5th and 7th notes can be used to create a variety of chords. What about the other three notes from the scale – the 2nd, 4th and 6th? These can also be used to produce chords.

The major 6th can be added to a major triad to create a SIXTH chord. Adding the same note to a minor triad creates a MINOR SIXTH chord.

ADDING THE SECOND

This is in fact something of a misnomer since in practice it is invariably the compound equivalent of the 2nd – the 9th – that is used. Adding the 9th note to a triad produces what is known as an ADDED NINTH (this should not be confused with a pure NINTH chord which you will encounter in a moment). In practice, the added ninth chord is often played without the 3rd note.

It is also possible to add the 9th note to a minor triad. This produces a MINOR ADDED NINTH. This chord is unusual in that the interval between the 2nd (9th) note and the flattened 3rd note is a minor 2nd (or semitone), making it a dissonant interval. Nonetheless, these chords are widely used.

All chords that add a 9th to a triad of any kind are usually abbreviated to "add nines".

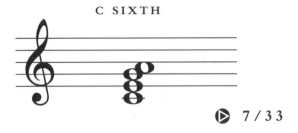

C SIXTH

7 / 33

C MINOR SIXTH

7 / 34

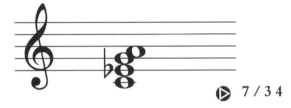

C ADDED NINTH

7 / 35

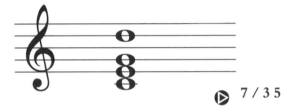

C MINOR ADDED NINTH

7 / 36

ABBREVIATING CHORD NAMES

∾∾∾∾

IN MANY FORMS OF MODERN MUSIC, ONLY THE BAREST FORMAL HARMONIC OUTLINES ARE USED. THIS CAN OFTEN MEAN THAT ALL A MUSICIAN HAS TO WORK FROM IS A SET OF CHORDS THAT CAN BE PLAYED ANY WAY THEY WISH. IN THESE CASES, THE CHORDS ARE NOT EVEN NECESSARILY NOTATED ON A MUSICAL STAFF, BUT SIMPLY WRITTEN OUT ON A CHART USING ABBREVIATED NAMES FOR THE CHORDS. ON THE RIGHT YOU WILL FIND A LIST OF THE MOST COMMONLY USED CHORDS ALONG WITH THEIR 'SHORTHAND" NAMES. EXAMPLES ARE SHOWN WITH C AS THE ROOT NOTE.

C MAJOR	C MAJ OR C
C MINOR	C MIN OR Cm
C DOMINANT SEVENTH	C7
C MINOR SEVENTH	C MIN 7 OR Cm7
C MAJOR SEVENTH	C MAJ 7 OR CΔ7
C HALF-DIMINISHED	C MIN 7-5 OR Cm7-5
C DIMINISHED	C DIM OR C°
C AUGMENTED	C AUG OR C+
C SUSPENDED FOURTH	C SUS OR C SUS 4
C SIXTH	C6
C MINOR SIXTH	C MIN 6 OR Cm6
C ADDED NINTH	C ADD 9
C NINTH	C9
C ELEVEN	C11
C THIRTEEN	C13

ADDING THE FOURTH

Chords that make use of the 4th note have a less usual role in that they are not added to an existing triad or chord. When the perfect 4th is used it traditionally REPLACES the 3rd note in a triad. For example, in the key of C major, the notes C (I), F (IV) and G (V) are used. This effect creates what is referred to as a SUSPENDED FOURTH chord. Such chords are are usually abbreviated to "sus four" after the note name, or even simply "suspended".

An alternative form of suspended chord makes a similar movement from the 3rd note to the 4th note in a dominant seventh chord. This effect is known as a SEVENTH SUSPENDED FOURTH chord, or "seven sus four". They are sometimes abbreviated as simply "7+4".

Suspended fourth chords can be heard in all forms of music and are usually resolved by shifting the 4th note back to the 3rd note at the end of a musical phrase. An example of this effect using both types of suspended chord is shown on the staff below. In each case the suspended note is returns to the major 3rd creating a major triad and dominant seventh chord respectively.

▶ 7/37

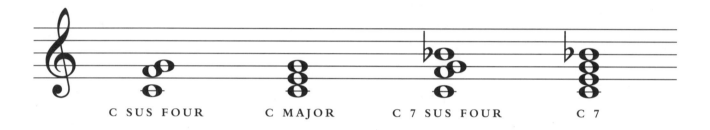

C SUS FOUR   C MAJOR   C 7 SUS FOUR   C 7

EXTENDED CHORDS

Compound intervals can be used to create a wide variety of full-sounding voicings with the addition of 9th, 11th and 13th intervals. These are known as EXTENDED CHORDS.

A NINTH chord is so named because it adds a compound interval of a 9th (that's a 2nd plus an octave) to a seventh chord. As there are a variety of seventh chords, there also be a range of ninths. The most common – simply known as a "ninth" – adds the 9th note to a dominant seventh chord. The two other commonly used forms of this group are the minor and major ninths, which add the same note to minor seventh and major seventh chords respectively.

ELEVENTH and THIRTEENTH notes work in exactly the same way. The eleventh set of chords add the perfect 4th note above the octave to a ninth chord; the thirteenth set of chords adds the major 6th above the octave to the eleventh.

When played in its fullest form, a ninth chord will comprise five notes; the eleventh has six notes; and the thirteenth has seven notes. However, it isn't imperative that all of the notes are played to give the a flavour of the extension.

C NINTH

▶ 7/38

C ELEVENTH

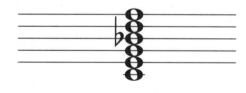

▶ 7/39

C THIRTEENTH

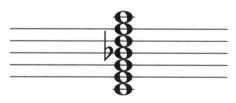

▶ 7/40

PLAYING WITH THE BASS NOTES

If you take a triad or chord and invert the notes you alter the balance of the notes and hence the way it sounds. From the composers of the great orchestral works to the thrashiest of modern pop and rock bands, all have learned that crucial changes in texture and impact can be achieved by the simplest of inversions.

On this page we will look at the way in which the sound of a chord can be changed by altering the bass note – using a note other than the root. When other notes from the chord are used in this way, they are effectively inversions, although in informal chord abbreviations they are usually notated as the chord name followed by a stroke and then the bass note. For example, the second chord shown below, "G/B", indicates a G major chord is being played over a bass note of B.

The staves below show four simple G major triads being played over bass notes taken from the triad itself, although played in a lower register. You can hear this effect on the CD.   ▶ 7 / 41

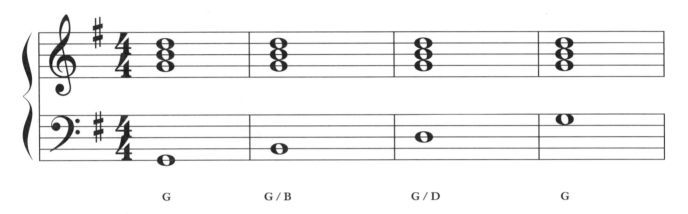

G   G / B   G / D   G

POLYTONAL EFFECTS

When two different chord types are played at the same time, the result is called a POLYTONAL CHORD (or simply a "polychord"). For example, if you take a C major triad (C-E-G) and play it with a G major triad (G-B-D), the result is the combination of C-E-G-B-D, which is the C ninth chord.

A polytonal effect can be created by playing a chord which adds a bass note from outside of the triad. This is not technically a polychord because it only uses the root note, but it is a widely used effect.

The staff below contains five commonly used chords with altered bass notes. To make comparison easier, the bass note is the same in each case but is different in relation to notes of each successive triad.

Although these chords are labelled as a triad with a bass note specified after the stroke, like the C ninth example shown earlier, they can also be given a new chord name based on the three notes of the triad in relation to the bass notes. For example, D major (D-F♯-A) played over C when viewed as a C chord is made from the notes C (1st), D (major 2nd/9th), F♯ (augmented 4th) and A (major 6th). Such a chord could also be termed C 6/9+4. The five altered-bass chords are shown below alongside their extended names.   ▶ 7 / 42

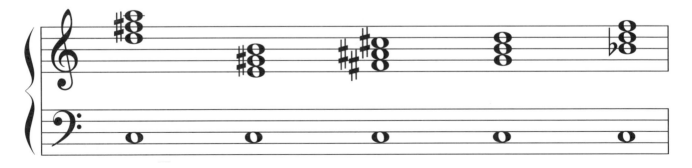

D / C   E / C   F♯ / C   G / C   B♭ / C

ARPEGGIOS

On page 71 you practised breaking down triads into their component parts. This is the basis of a widely used playing effect known as an ARPEGGIO, an instruction to play a chord as a quick succession of notes. That the term derives from the Italian word for harp gives a clue to the way the effect sounds.

An arpeggio can be shown in several different ways – the top three examples on the right are all valid possibilities. The example beneath them shows how the effect could be written out in "long hand".

▶ 7 / 43

BROKEN CHORDS

Similar to the arpeggio is the BROKEN CHORD in which the constituent notes are played as a rhythmic pattern. Broken chords are often used by pianists as a part of regular practice.

One of the best-known musical uses of broken chords is in what is called the ALBERTI BASS. This is specific pattern that breaks a triad into single notes which are then played in a sequence that moves 1st note, 5th note, 3rd note and 5th note. Popularized by the 18th-century Italian composer Domenico Alberti (1710-40), its most famous use is in Mozart's "Sonata in C Major (K.545)".

The example below illustrates that the pattern on the first staff is clearly derived from the chords shown on the second staff.   ▶ 7 / 44

TIME OUT: SUMMARY OF LESSON 7

∼∼∼∼

HERE IS A SUMMARY OF THE MAJOR POINTS SHOWN IN THIS LESSON.

- MAJOR, MINOR, DIMINISHED AND AUGMENTED TRIADS
- TRIADS ON THE MAJOR AND MINOR SCALES
- INVERTING TRIADS
- THE OPEN AND CLOSE POSITION
- CHORDS AND THEIR INVERSIONS

- CONSTRUCTING SEVENTH CHORDS
- ADDING THE 2ND, 4TH AND 6TH NOTES
- EXTENDING CHORDS USING THE 9TH, 11TH AND 13TH NOTES
- ALTERED BASS NOTES AND POLYCHORDS
- ARPEGGIOS AND BROKEN CHORDS

LESSON 8:

Groups and Phrases

Notes with a value of a quaver or less can be shown grouped together on the staff using beams or ties. This makes music easier to read and enables the musician to recognize quickly certain types of rhythmic pattern. However, as you will have discovered, there are many different ways to achieve the same end result using standard music notation, so it is useful to understand the most appropriate practices.

GROUPINGS

You've already seen the way in which notes can be grouped together using beams or ties. Just to remind you, the two staves on the right (above) represent the same set of note values. The beamed version is easier to read and provides a natural grouping for the notes. When the note values within the group are mixed, beaming can still be used.

FIXED NOTE GROUPS

MIXED NOTE GROUPS

TRIPLET DIVISIONS

All the note value examples used so far have operated on the premise that the subdivision of notes was based on a factor of two – that is, they could be halved, quartered and so forth. However, a beat can also be divided into three equal parts. The beats that result are known as TRIPLETS. Every type of note can be divided in this way.

There are several methods for notating triplets. The options shown on the right are all equally legitimate (and are not exclusive to those note values) and their use is largely down to personal taste. However in each case, the principle is exactly the same. In the example immediately to the right, the instruction is for the three quavers to be played in the same amount of time that it takes to play a crotchet. You can hear the effect of a triplet chord played over a metronome beat on the CD.   ▶ 8 / 1

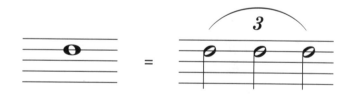

MINIM TRIPLETS

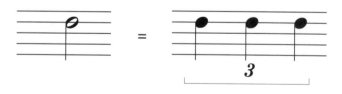

CROTCHET TRIPLETS

QUAVER TRIPLETS

TRIPLET GROUPINGS

Although it is the most common way in which they are used, a triplet division does not necessarily mean that three notes of equal value will be produced. It is also possible to create groups of mixed triplets made up from notes and rests of different values. Four examples are shown on the right.

If a piece of music makes extensive use of triplets throughout the number "3" is sometimes dropped from the score. However, it's reasonable to say that such heavy use of triplets is relatively unusual within a simple time signature – it would be more usual for the piece to be written in the equivalent compound time signature. The example below illustrates the same

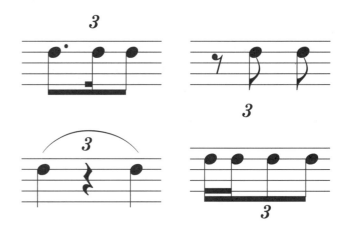

bar notated in four-four (simple time) and its compound equivalent – twelve-eight. Both bars sound identical when played.   ▶ 8 / 2

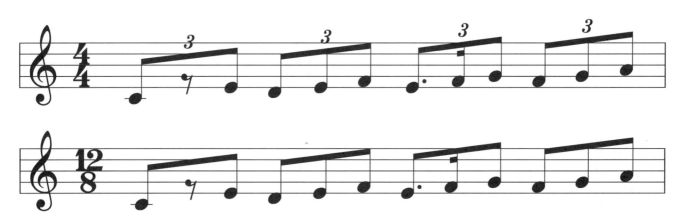

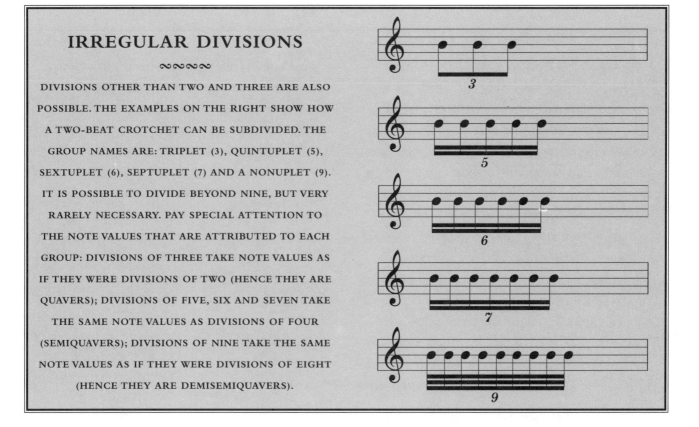

IRREGULAR DIVISIONS

∞∞∞

DIVISIONS OTHER THAN TWO AND THREE ARE ALSO POSSIBLE. THE EXAMPLES ON THE RIGHT SHOW HOW A TWO-BEAT CROTCHET CAN BE SUBDIVIDED. THE GROUP NAMES ARE: TRIPLET (3), QUINTUPLET (5), SEXTUPLET (6), SEPTUPLET (7) AND A NONUPLET (9). IT IS POSSIBLE TO DIVIDE BEYOND NINE, BUT VERY RARELY NECESSARY. PAY SPECIAL ATTENTION TO THE NOTE VALUES THAT ARE ATTRIBUTED TO EACH GROUP: DIVISIONS OF THREE TAKE NOTE VALUES AS IF THEY WERE DIVISIONS OF TWO (HENCE THEY ARE QUAVERS); DIVISIONS OF FIVE, SIX AND SEVEN TAKE THE SAME NOTE VALUES AS DIVISIONS OF FOUR (SEMIQUAVERS); DIVISIONS OF NINE TAKE THE SAME NOTE VALUES AS IF THEY WERE DIVISIONS OF EIGHT (HENCE THEY ARE DEMISEMIQUAVERS).

GROUPING PROTOCOL

By now you will be sufficiently familiar with the way notes are grouped on a staff to know that there are any number of ways in which the same patterns can be notated. Written music is all about communicating a composer or arranger's idea to the performer and as such, ANY system that gets the information across accurately or unambiguously has to be valid. That said, however, some notation techniques are better than others.

When grouping notes together, the golden rule to observe is the minimization of ties. Whilst there is no sensible alternative to using ties when sustaining notes across bar lines, if they are overused within bars – for example, using a tie between a minim and a crotchet instead of dotting the minim (which *is* an alternative that any sightreader would be able to understand) – they make the score more difficult to read. Moreover, ties can easily be confused with articulation marks such as slurs (see page 86).

SENSIBLE PRACTICE

In most simple-time uses, ties within a bar can be avoided by using dotted notes. Here are some basic examples that emphasize this point. In each instance the undesirable version is shown on the left.

BEAMING STANDARDS

∽∽∽∽

THE BEAMING OF QUAVERS AND SMALLER VALUES ALSO HAS ITS OWN SET OF RULES. IN REGULAR USE, QUAVERS SHOULD BE BEAMED EITHER IN GROUPS OF TWO, FOUR OR (IN THREE-FOUR TIME) SIX. THIS MEANS THAT IN A TWO-FOUR OR THREE-FOUR BAR OF QUAVERS THE ENTIRE BAR CAN BE BEAMED. IN THREE-FOUR TIME IT'S BEST TO AVOID BEAMING GROUPS OF THREE QUAVERS UNLESS THEY ARE TRIPLETS, WHICH MAY IMPLY THE COMPOUND TIME OF SIX-EIGHT. THE STANDARD PRACTICE IS TO PULL ONE OF THE QUAVERS OUT OF THE GROUP LEAVING A PAIR THAT PLAY ON THE BEAT (SEE RIGHT). WHEN ATTACHING BEAMS IN FOUR-FOUR TIME YOU SHOULD THINK OF THE BAR AS BEING DIVIDED INTO A PAIR OF TWO-BEAT UNITS – BEAMING CANNOT TAKE PLACE ACROSS THAT DIVIDE. THUS, FOUR QUAVERS APPEARING IN THE MIDDLE OF THE BAR SHOULD NOT BE BEAMED BUT SHOWN AS TWO PAIRS OF TWO (SEE FOOT OF THE PAGE).

VALUES LESS THAN A QUAVER CAN BE BEAMED ON THE BEAT OR THE HALF-BEAT. THUS IN FOUR-FOUR TIME THERE SHOULD NEVER BE MORE THAN FOUR SEMIQUAVERS GROUPED, BUT IT WOULD ACCEPTABLE TO SHOW EIGHT DEMISEMIQUAVERS.

UNDESIRABLE   DESIRABLE

TEST 27

LOOK AT THE PIECE OF MUSIC SHOWN BELOW. ALTHOUGH IT "WORKS" (WITH THE EXCEPTION OF ONE SERIOUS ERROR), THERE ARE A NUMBER OF WAYS IN WHICH THE NOTATION COULD BE RADICALLY IMPROVED. THIS EXERCISE HAS BEEN DELIBERATELY WRITTEN IN AN AWKWARD KEY, SO WHILE YOU REWORK THE NOTATION, MARK DOWN THE NOTE NAMES – REMEMBER, ONLY PRACTICE WILL IMPROVE YOUR SIGHTREADING SKILLS.

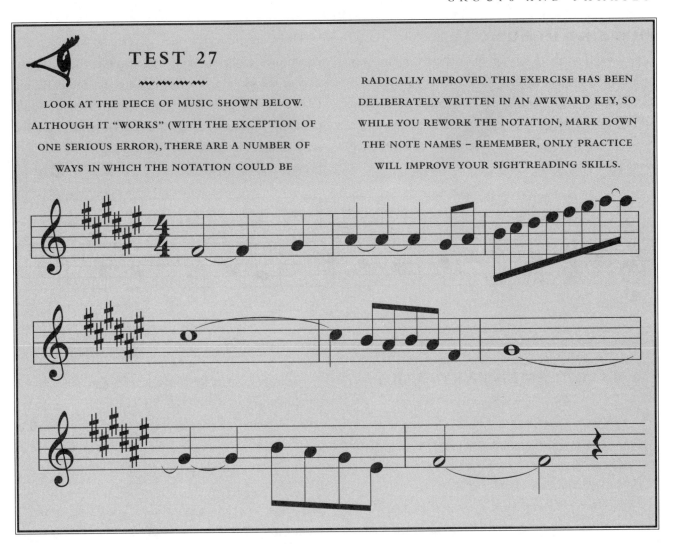

GROUPING RESTS

There is also protocol for the way in which rests are grouped. The rule-of-thumb is that wherever possible they should be positioned on the beat. For example, in a bar of two-four whose only note is a quaver on the last half-beat, for the sake of clarity, the first beat of the bar should be a crotchet rest; the second beat of the bar can be made up with a quaver rest.

The example on the right shows two undesirable alternatives followed by the "correct" option. The top example begins with a half-beat rest followed by a whole-beat rest. This is not ideal because the rests as they are shown cut across the beats – the whole-beat rest begins on the half-beat and ends on one-and-a-half beats.

The second alternative shows a dotted rest. Like dotted notes, all of the rests may have their value increased by half in the same manner. Dotted rests, however, are only really appropriate in compound time where the basic beat is a dotted crotchet.

UNDESIRABLE

UNDESIRABLE

DESIRABLE

PHRASING IN MUSIC

A reasonable analogy can be made between the way in which we speak and the way in which music is composed. Just as speech can be broken down into self-contained paragraphs and sentences so too can a piece of music. The musical equivalent of a sentence is referred to as a PHRASE.

There are no strict rules governing what actually constitutes a phrase. Take, for example, the first four bars of the children's song "London Bridge Is Falling Down", shown below. The staves shown would certainly constitute a phrase, but it could also be argued that the first two bars are also a phrase in their own right.   ▶ 8 / 3

COMPLEMENTARY BARS

∽∾∽∾

YOU WILL FIND THAT OFTEN PIECES OF MUSIC DON'T ACTUALLY BEGIN ON THE FIRST BEAT OF THE FIRST BAR. THIS RESULTS IN WHAT SEEMS TO BE INCORRECT BAR LENGTHS. THE EXAMPLE BELOW – THE SONG "CLEMENTINE" – HAS THE FIRST TWO NOTES STARTING ON THE THE FINAL BEAT OF A BAR. SO CAN IT BE CORRECT FOR A BAR OF THREE-FOUR TIME TO CONTAIN NOTE VALUES THAT DO NOT TOTAL THREE BEATS? SHOULD WE PERHAPS STEP IN AND PLACE A PAIR OF CROTCHET RESTS ON BEATS ONE AND TWO? IN BOTH CASES THIS IS NOT NECESSARY. THE BEAT VALUES ARE BALANCED OVER THE ENTIRE PIECE OF MUSIC. NOTICE THAT FINAL BAR CONTAINS A MINIM WORTH TWO BEATS. THIS COMPLEMENTS THE SINGLE BEAT TAKEN UP AT THE BEGINNING. AS YOU PROBABLY KNOW, THIS SONG HAS A NUMBER OF OTHER VERSES WHICH WILL ALSO BEGIN ON WHAT COULD BE SEEN AS THE FINAL BEAT OF THE FINAL BAR. IN FACT, IF THE FINAL BAR CONTAINED A DOTTED MINIM (OR A MINIM AND CROTCHET REST) AN EXTRA BEAT WOULD BE ADDED BETWEEN VERSES, WHICH WOULD CLEARLY BE WRONG. THIS SAME SENSE OF BALANCE IS TRUE OF ALL MUSICAL PHRASES. THE FIRST LINE OF THE SONG (SHOWN BRACKETED) CONSTITUTES A PHRASE IN ITS OWN RIGHT. INDEED, THIS IS INVARIABLY TRUE WITH ANY SONG. NOTICE THAT ALTHOUGH THE PHRASE DOESN'T BEGIN OR END ON THE BAR, IT REMAINS PERFECTLY BALANCED IN TERMS OF THE TIME VALUES.   ▶ 8 / 4

OH MY   DAR-LING, OH MY   DAR-LING, OH MY   DAR-LING CLEM-EN-TINE,   THOU ART

LOST   AND   GONE   FOR-EV-ER   DREAD-FUL   SOR-RY   CLEM-EN-TINE.

ARTICULATION MARKS

Defining a musical phrase has a practical value in steering the performance of a piece of music. A phrase can be shown formally using ARTICULATION MARKS, in particular a symbol called a SLUR. A curved line which is not dissimilar in appearance to a tie, a slur can be placed around a phrase of any length, be it two bars or two notes.

A defining characteristic of a phrase is a brief pause at its end. When we speak we usually end a phrase within a sentence or paragraph with a natural pause. It is the same in written music. A slur placed around a phrase has the practical effect of shortening the final note within its boundary, thus emphasizing the self-contained nature of the grouping.

The example below illustrates this point. On the upper staff there are three slurs, each one ending on a quaver. On the lower staff each of the end quavers has been replaced by a semiquaver and a semiquaver rest, thus creating the effect of a natural pause. Notice that the link between the minim and the crotchet is NOT a slur but a tie.

Implicit within the boundaries of a slur is the requirement to play the notes in a smooth and flowing manner, creating a cohesion that once again emphasizes the "togetherness" of the phrase. This is known as LEGATO. Notes within the slur MUST be played without any breaks.

In the hands of a good musician the interpretation of the slur is subtle and can't be defined in such strict terms as halving note values. Indeed, the term "feel" is probably as good as any to describe a process aimed at making the music sound as natural as possible.

> ## CADENCES
> ∾∾∾
> MUSICAL PHRASES END WITH WHAT IS KNOWN AS A <u>CADENCE</u>. THIS DESCRIBES THE MUSICAL EFFECT THAT OCCURS AT THE END OF PHRASE – AT THE END OF MOST PIECES OF MUSIC THIS USUALLY MEANS A RETURN TO THE TONIC CHORD. THE MOST COMMON TYPE IS THE <u>PERFECT CADENCE</u> WHICH DESCRIBES A RESOLUTION FROM THE DOMINANT (V) TO THE TONIC (I). AN <u>IMPERFECT CADENCE</u> USUALLY DESCRIBES A MOVEMENT FROM THE TONIC (I) TO THE DOMINANT (V). CREATING A TEMPORARY FEEL, THE IMPERFECT CADENCE RARELY ENDS A MAJOR PASSAGE. THE <u>PLAGAL CADENCE</u> MOVES FROM THE SUBDOMINANT (IV) TO THE TONIC (I) – THINK, FOR EXAMPLE, OF THE "AMEN" SUNG AT THE END OF HYMN. FINALLY, AN <u>INTERRUPTED CADENCE</u> IS A MOVEMENT FROM THE DOMINANT (V) TO ANY DEGREE OTHER THAN THE TONIC (I) – USUALLY THE SUBMEDIANT.

> ## TIME OUT: SUMMARY OF LESSON 8
> ∾∾∾
> HERE IS A SUMMARY OF THE TOPICS COVERED IN THIS LESSON.
>
> • TRIPLETS AND OTHER IRREGULAR DIVISIONS   • RULES OF BEAMING
> • GROUPING NOTES   • RECOGNIZING PHRASES
> • GROUPING RESTS   • ARTICULATION AND SLURS

LESSON 9:

Non-Diatonic Scales

The diatonic scales that make up the major and minor series are the most widely used in most forms of Western music. However, there are a number of other scale types made up from different combinations of intervals of the twelve semitone steps between the octave. These are known as SYNTHETIC scales. Among this group are the major and minor pentatonic, chromatic, diminished and whole-tone scale series.

PENTATONIC SCALES

Among the most widely used synthetic scale types, pentatonic scales are among the oldest known. Variations have been found in the diverse ethnic musical cultures of Asia, the Far East and Native America. As the name suggests, pentatonic scales are built using five notes. The two forms most likely to be used are the MAJOR PENTATONIC and the MINOR PENTATONIC scales.

THE MINOR PENTATONIC SCALE

Minor pentatonic scales are very widely used in blues, jazz and rock as a basis for soloing. Indeed, such is its use in these fields that the minor pentatonic scale is often referred to as the "blues" scale. The scale takes its notes from the natural minor except that it leaves out the 2nd and 6th notes. The unique set of intervals follows the pattern TONE PLUS SEMITONE-TONE-TONE-TONE PLUS SEMITONE-TONE. In the key of C, the notes used are C, E♭, F, G and B♭.

It is possible to create a set of five scales by starting from different positions on the minor pentatonic. Using the notes from the key of C, pentatonic scales can also be played using the patterns E♭-F-G-B♭-C; F-G-B♭-C-E♭; G-B♭-C-E♭-F; and B♭-C-E♭-F-B. As you can see, the notes are the same in each case but the pattern of intervals is different and thus so is its sound. These are called PENTATONIC MODES. A full set of all five minor pentatonic modes can be heard on the CD in the key of C. ▶ 9 / 1

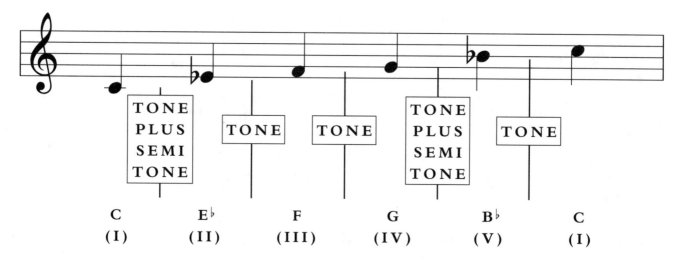

THE MAJOR PENTATONIC

The second principle pentatonic scale, the major pentatonic scale uses the same notes as the regular diatonic major scale except that it leaves out the 4th and 7th notes. The unique set of intervals follows the pattern TONE-TONE-TONE PLUS SEMITONE-TONE-TONE PLUS SEMITONE. Thus, in the key of C, the notes used are C, D, E, G and A.

As with all other scales, this set of intervals can be transposed to every key.

▶ 9 / 2

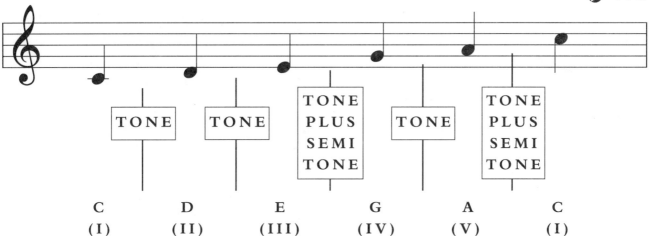

	TONE	TONE	TONE PLUS SEMI TONE	TONE	TONE PLUS SEMI TONE	
C (I)		D (II)		E (III)		G (IV)		A (V)		C (I)

CHROMATIC SCALE

∞∞∞∞

A CHROMATIC SCALE IS ONE THAT COMPRISES ALL THE SEMITONES WITHIN AN OCTAVE. THIS MEANS THAT THERE ARE TWELVE EQUAL INTERVALS BETWEEN THE TONIC AND THE OCTAVE. PRACTICAL USE OF CHROMATIC NOTES IN MUSIC HAS TENDED TOWARDS TWO DISTINCT FORMS: ORNAMENTAL– AS "EFFECTS" IN TONAL MUSIC – OR STRUCTURAL – IN THE CREATION OF TONALLY AMBIGUOUS (OR EVEN ATONAL) MUSICAL WORKS.

CHROMATIC NOTES HAVE BEEN USED IN MUSIC SINCE THE DIATONIC SYSTEM BECAME DOMINANT IN THE LATE 16TH CENTURY. IN SUCH SITUATIONS THEY HAVE OFTEN BEEN USED DECORATIVELY, FOR EXAMPLE AS PASSING NOTES, "FILLING" IN THE GAPS BETWEEN INTERVALS OF A TONE. DURING THIS TIME, HOWEVER, IN SPITE OF THESE ADDITIONAL NOTES A SENSE OF TONALITY WAS USUALLY MAINTAINED – THAT IS, THE MUSIC COULD ALWAYS BE IDENTIFIED AS BEING IN AN IDENTIFIABLE KEY.

EXTENSIVE USE OF CHROMATICISM IN THE COMPOSITION OF MUSIC BEGAN TOWARDS THE END OF THE 19TH CENTURY. THIS GREW TO THE POINT THAT BY THE BEGINNING OF THE CENTURY THAT FOLLOWED TONAL MUSIC HAD BECOME LARGELY UNFASHIONABLE AMONG SERIOUS COMPOSERS. THIS MOVEMENT SAW THE BIRTH OF A NEW COMPOSITIONAL FORM – THE TWELVE-TONE SYSTEM. THE MOST NOTED PIONEER OF THIS NEW APPROACH WAS THE GERMAN COMPOSER ARNOLD SCHOENBERG, WHO CREATED A "SERIAL MUSIC" THAT COULD DRAW EQUALLY ON ALL TWELVE NOTES OF THE CHROMATIC SCALE WITHOUT THERE BEING A TONAL CENTRE OR KEY.

THE STAFF BELOW SHOWS A ONE-OCTAVE CHROMATIC SCALE BETWEEN TWO "C" NOTES. THE SCALE WOULD BE IDENTICAL ON WHATEVER NOTE IT WAS STARTED. ▶ 9 / 3

THE DIMINISHED SCALE

The diminished scale comprises eight intervals that alternate between between tones and semitones. The consistency of these intervals means that the same pattern can be started from four different points with-in the scale – the 1st, 3rd, 5th and 7th degrees. Thus with four tonal centres, it becomes possible to build scales for all keys and their enharmonic equivalents from just three sets of notes.   ▶ 9 / 4

I	II	III	IV	V	VI	VII	VIII
C̲	D	E̲♭	F	G̲♭	G♯	A̲	B
C̲♯	D♯	E̲	F♯	G̲	A	B̲♭	C
D̲	E	F̲	G	A̲♭	B♭	B̲	C♯

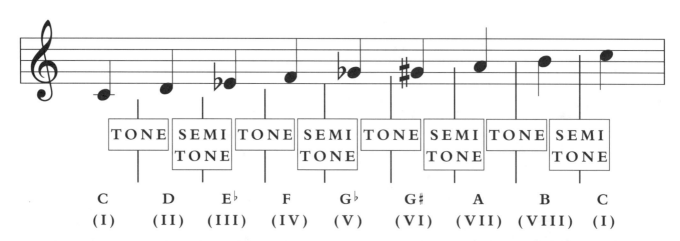

C (I) D (II) E♭ (III) F (IV) G♭ (V) G♯ (VI) A (VII) B (VIII) C (I)

TONE SEMI TONE TONE SEMI TONE TONE SEMI TONE TONE SEMI TONE

AN ALTERNATIVE DIMINISHED SCALE
∾∾∾∾

IT IS POSSIBLE TO PLAY THE DIMINISHED SCALE BY REVERSING THE PATTERN OF INTERVALS – STARTING WITH AN INTERVAL OF A SEMITONE INSTEAD OF A TONE. TO SEE HOW THIS WORKS, LOOK AT THE TABLE OF KEY CENTRES ON THE LEFT AND CREATE SCALES STARTING ON THE NOTES THAT ARE <u>NOT</u> UNDERLINED. AS BEFORE, THE THREE SETS OF NOTES ARE ALL YOU NEED TO CREATE THESE DIMINISHED SCALES IN EVERY KEY.

ETHNIC SCALES
∾∾∾∾

THE SIX EXAMPLES SHOWN ON THE RIGHT ARE WESTERNIZED VERSIONS OF ETHNIC SCALES USED IN THE MUSIC OF EASTERN EUROPE, CENTRAL AND SOUTHEAST ASIA AND THE FAR EAST. THEY CAN BE USED TO PROVIDE A FLAVOUR OF THE SOUNDS OF THESE CULTURES, SOME OF WHOM DO NOT USE CHROMATIC TUNING – THAT IS, THEIR INDIGENOUS MUSICAL SYSTEMS DO NOT NECESSARILY DIVIDE AN OCTAVE INTO TWELVE EQUAL PARTS LIKE WE DO IN THE WEST. INDEED, WHEN SUCH SCALES ARE PLAYED IN THEIR ORIGINAL FORMS THEY CAN SOUND ALIEN OR SIMPLY "WRONG" TO WESTERN EARS. EVEN THESE APPROXIMATIONS, SOME OF WHICH HAVE AN UNDENIABLY DISSONANT FLAVOUR, WOULD BE CONSIDERED "DIFFICULT" BY MANY LISTENERS.

PELOG SCALE   ▶ 9 / 5

INDIAN SCALE   ▶ 9 / 6

HIRAJOSHI SCALE   ▶ 9 / 7

KUMOI SCALE   ▶ 9 / 8

NEAPOLITAN SCALE   ▶ 9 / 9

HUNGARIAN SCALE   ▶ 9 / 10

THE WHOLE-TONE SCALE

Also known as the augmented scale, the WHOLE-TONE scale is so named because it moves from the the root to the octave over the course of six tones. Hence, the pattern of intervals is TONE-TONE-TONE-TONE-TONE-TONE.

Like the chromatic scale, although the whole-tone system was in use before the start of the 20th century, it was only at this time that composers such as Debussy and most notably Messiaen created works based entirely around its use.

As each of the intervals is identical, the effect of the scale will sound the same irrespective of the starting note. This means that there are only two different combinations of notes needed to play an augmented scale in any key. The version shown below uses the notes C-D-E-F#-G#-A#; the alternative uses the same scale raised by a semitone (C#-D#-F-G-A-B).

Notice that because there is no key centre in the diatonic sense the enharmonic notes within the whole-tone scale can be named according to preference or convenience. ▶ 9/11

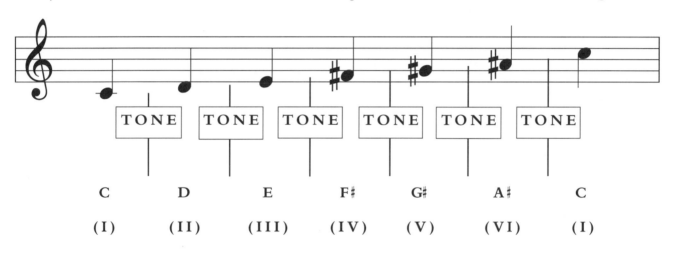

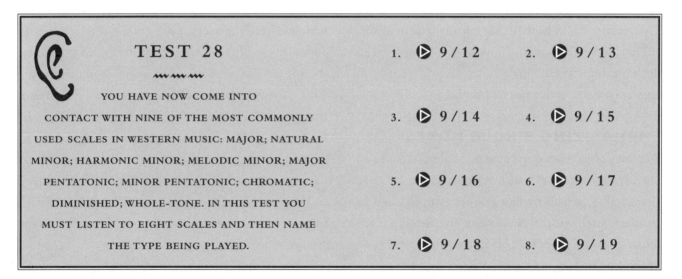

TEST 28

YOU HAVE NOW COME INTO CONTACT WITH NINE OF THE MOST COMMONLY USED SCALES IN WESTERN MUSIC: MAJOR; NATURAL MINOR; HARMONIC MINOR; MELODIC MINOR; MAJOR PENTATONIC; MINOR PENTATONIC; CHROMATIC; DIMINISHED; WHOLE-TONE. IN THIS TEST YOU MUST LISTEN TO EIGHT SCALES AND THEN NAME THE TYPE BEING PLAYED.

1. ▶ 9/12   2. ▶ 9/13

3. ▶ 9/14   4. ▶ 9/15

5. ▶ 9/16   6. ▶ 9/17

7. ▶ 9/18   8. ▶ 9/19

TIME OUT: SUMMARY OF LESSON 9

HERE IS A SUMMARY OF THE MAJOR POINTS SHOWN IN THIS LESSON.

• THE MAJOR PENTATONIC SCALE
• THE MINOR PENTATONIC SCALE
• THE CHROMATIC SCALE

• THE DIMINISHED SCALES
• ETHNIC SCALES
• THE WHOLE-TONE OR AUGMENTED SCALE

LESSON 10:

Performance Issues

In purely mechanical terms, music is created by bringing together notes of differing pitches and differing lengths. But there is a further crucial element – volume. If every note was played with exactly the same dynamic, imagine how dull music would sound. The same can also be said of tempo. Performance effects can be added to a manuscript to provide the musician with instructions as to how the piece should be played.

DYNAMICS

Think about of way in which groups of people engage in conversation. To create impact or other desired effects, we emphasise certain words or phrases by speaking at a higher volume. This enables us to communicate our views or feelings more accurately. This process of DYNAMICS is equally true of music.

Dynamic effects within music can be applied at three distinct levels: single-note; musical phrase or segment; or the entire piece of music.

EMPHASIZING SINGLE NOTES

You have already seen a simple example of how playing certain notes at a higher volume can be used effectively to create rhythm and feel within a bar of crotchets, each with an equal value on page 46. In this instance an ACCENT MARK was used. This is an instruction to play the note louder by positioning the symbol "Λ" above the note or "V" below the note). Another valid accent mark is the symbol ">", which can be placed either above or below the music. Although they are often used in an interchangeable fashion, there is a prevailing view that the symbol ">" has a milder effect than "Λ" or "V".

Using such an ambivalent term as "mild" above provides a further illustration of the discretionary nature of music performance. Unlike their electronic counterparts, there is no empirical way of regulating the volumes of standard acoustic musical instruments. Thus, accent marks could be viewed as little more than an instruction to "play this note a bit louder". In truth, the effect is much more subtle. Their use will depend on the musical context – the way in which they are interpreted is largely a matter of the quality and experience of the performer. What it DOESN'T mean, though, is that accented notes should be played as loud as possible.

This example shows accenting on alternate chords. To emphasize the effect, you can hear it played with accents and then without. ▶ 10 / 1

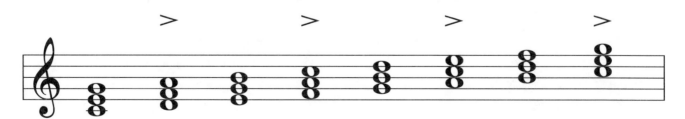

WRITTEN INSTRUCTIONS

Just as tempos can be indicated by specific words written on the score (see page 49), so too can volume. These revolve around the use of a series of Italian words based around *piano* (meaning "soft") and *forte* (meaning "loud"). If we bring those two words together it gives us "pianoforte", which technically the correct name for the piano.

When written on a score these descriptions are usually abbreviated in a stylized script and positioned above or between the staves. The symbol used to show *piano* is ***p***; the symbol used to show *forte* is ***f***. These two letters can be grouped together in various ways. An instruction to play louder than *forte* is *fortissimo*, shown as ***ff***. If it is required to be louder still then the *fortississimo* symbol (***fff***) is used. Further *forte*

symbols can be added – some composers have used as many as six – although these are quite rare. The same process can be applied to the *piano* instruction (see panel below).

As the differences between each successive grade is quite subtle, we can reasonably say that rather than giving the performer literal and explicit instructions, dynamic marks need to be interpreted with the mood of the piece of music in mind.

An example of how this works is shown in the staves below – a sequence from one of Beethoven's piano sonatas. Notice that at the end of the fourth bar there is an instruction to play *forte* which carries through to the end of the seventh bar, when once again it returns to *piano*. This remains the default until the next dynamic mark.

DYNAMIC MARKS

∿∿∿∿

THE LIST BELOW SHOWS SOME OF THE MOST COMMONLY FOUND DYNAMIC MARKS
USED IN WRITTEN MUSIC.

ITALIAN NAME	DESCRIPTION	ABBREVIATION
FORTE	LOUD	*f*
PIANO	SOFT	*p*
MEZZO-FORTE	MEDIUM LOUD	*mf*
MEZZO-PIANO	MEDIUM SOFT	*mp*
FORTISSIMO	VERY LOUD	*ff*
FORTISSISSIMO	EXTREMELY LOUD	*fff*
PIANISSIMO	VERY SOFT	*pp*
PIANISSISSIMO	EXTREMELY SOFT	*ppp*
FORTE PIANO	LOUD THEN IMMEDIATELY SOFT	*fp*
POCO FORTE	SLIGHTLY LOUD	*pf*
SFORZATO/SFORZANDO	PLAYED WITH FORCE	*sf*
RINFORZATO/RINFORZANDO	BECOMING STRONGER	*rf*
SMORZANDO	GRADUALLY FADING	*smorz*
CALANDO	SLOWER WITH DECREASING VOLUME	*cal*

GRADUAL CHANGES IN VOLUME

Frequently within a piece of music volume changes take effect over a period of time or a group of notes. To take account of such occurrences, the *Crescendo* and *Diminuendo* (or *Decrescendo*) marks are used. *Crescendo* literally means "getting louder". *Diminuendo* translates as "getting softer". In written music they can either be indicated above the stave respectively as *cresc* and *dim,* or shown using the two "hairpin" symbols shown on the right.

If the changes in volume are to take place within the space of a few bars, the hairpin is stretched across those bars to indicate the point at which the volume begins to change and the point at which it ends.

One problem with using the hairpin symbols is that they don't, in themselves, tell the musicians how

CRESCENDO

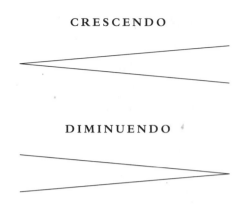

DIMINUENDO

loudly or softly they should be playing when they reach the end. This can in some ways be resolved by placing dynamic marks at the end of the symbol. The example below shows a *crescendo* over four bars in which time the volume has increased from *piano* to *fortissimo*.

▶ 10 / 2

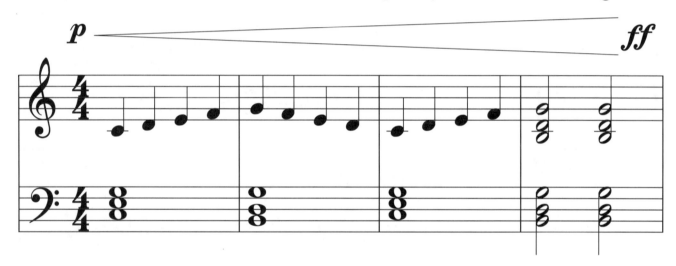

STACCATO

Literally meaning "short", the term STACCATO is an instruction to shorten the length of a note. Although there are a number ways it can be shown, the most common is the placement of a dot above the head of the note.

One problem with playing staccato is judging exactly how much shorter the note ought to be. It is, however, NOT an instruction to shorten the note as much as possible – to do that requires the performer to play *staccatissimo* (shown using the symbol ▲).

The examples on the right show how a bar of four staccato crotchets can be played as quavers or dotted quavers with rests. On the CD you can hear the first bar played without the staccato effect and then with the staccato effect.   ▶ 10 / 3

STACCATO BAR

SHORTENED EQUIVALENTS

EMBELLISHMENTS

There are a number of symbols or written instructions that may appear on a piece of music that do not give absolutely precise instructions as to how it should be performed. As such, it is left to the skills and interpretive abilities of the performer to make these decisions. In terms of classical music, occurrences like these are usually known as EMBELLISHMENTS. A selection of the most commonly used of these terms are shown over the next two pages.

THE ACCIACCATURA

In some pieces of music you will come across a note prefixed by another note printed in a much smaller script. This tiny note – referred to as a GRACE NOTE will either be an ACCIACCATURA or an APPOGIATURA.

The acciaccatura is shown with a stroke through the stem. It is sometimes known as a CRUSHED NOTE, which gives a fairly accurate reflection of how the note sounds when played. The acciaccatura can be interpreted in three different ways. It can be played just before the beat; on the beat but with the accent heavily placed on the main note; or at the same time as the main note only played staccato. This last method can, of course, only be used on instruments that can play more than one note at a time.

Irrespective of how the acciaccatura is interpreted, however – and this is an important point – its value is NEVER included as a part of the whole bar.

Here are two examples of the acciaccatura in use. The second bar uses a beamed group of notes. These are shown as semiquavers and should be played as quickly as possible. ▶ 10 / 4

THE APPOGIATURA

An appogiatura literally means "leaning". Although it appears to be similar to the acciaccatura (without the stroke), this description provides a clue to the way in which it differs. The note always falls on the beat before resolving to the principle note. In other words, the appogiatura does literally lean on the main note.

There are two problems the musician faces when dealing with the appogiatura. The first is that it can appear to be the same as an acciaccatura (for which strokes are not used religiously). Secondly, although the appogiatura is usually shown as a semiquaver it does not necessarily mean that it "eats" a semiquaver out of the principal note. An informal definition was created in the 18th century by C.P.E. Bach (son of J.S. Bach) who stated that the appogiatura was worth half the value of the principle note if it was divisible by two, and two-thirds if it was divisible by three. While this is a workable "rule" it cannot be applied rigidly – this generally remains a matter for the discretion of the performer.

The staff below shows an appogiatura used within the context of a chord. In this example, the grace note is ONLY linked to the highest notes of each chord (G in both cases). This means that on the beat it is NOT just the grace note that is played followed quickly by the chord, but the notes C, E and F. After half a beat (using the Bach formula) the F resolves to G while C and E are still being sustained. The second example shows the same chord played an octave higher. ▶ 10 / 5

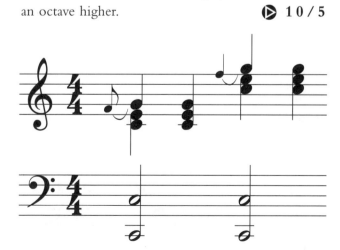

TRILLS AND MORDENTS

Sometimes also known as a "shake", a TRILL is a commonly used ornamental effect whereby a note is alternated at rapid speed with the next note above for that same key. Trills can be indicated either by placing the symbol "*tr*" above the note or a wavy line (some even show both methods). The example below shows how a trill placed above a crotchet C note could be interpreted.   ▶ 10 / 6

You'll notice that the last sentence was qualified with the word "could". In fact, the extent of the trill depends largely on the context of the music – in some cases it might even mean that only a single alternation was needed.

A MORDENT is an alternative type of trill in which the principal note alternates with the note BELOW. It is shown as a wavy line with a vertical stroke. The inverse effect is shown as a regular wavy line – the two forms are respectively referred to as UPPER and LOWER Mordents.

LOWER MORDENT   UPPER MORDENT

TURNS
∾∾∾∾

A TURN IS AN DECORATIVE EFFECT IN WHICH A SINGLE NOTE SHOWN WITH THE "SIDEWAYS S" SYMBOL IS PLAYED AS A FLOURISH USING THE TWO ADJACENT NOTES. IN THE EXAMPLE BELOW, A CROTCHET C CAN BE PLAYED AS D-C-B-C IN A GROUP OF SEMIQUAVERS. A SYMBOL APPEARING BETWEEN TWO NOTES MEANS THAT THE TURN MUST BE PERFORMED SO AS TO LEAD INTO THE SECOND GROUP.

TREMOLO

Throughout music history, the terms VIBRATO and TREMOLO have been used in an interchangeable fashion. In fact they create two very distinct effects.

Tremolo refers to the fast repetition of a single pitch. On string instruments the effect can be created by the rapid up-and-down motion of the bow against the strings; on the guitar by swift plectrum picking; on the piano by very fast depression of the key.

The tremolo can be shown using repeat stokes (below left). As you will see across the page, these symbols have other related uses.   ▶ 10 / 7

TREMOLO   ALTERNATIVE

VIBRATO

Vibrato is used by most string instruments and by the human voice. The effect is created by a slight though consistent variation in pitch which can create a full, rich sound, especially in an auditorium where the natural reverberation causes the pitches to blend.

String players and guitarists can create vibrato by rocking the left hand back and forth from the wrist. Wind players achieve the same effect by the careful regulation of the flow of breath. Vibrato cannot be achieved using instruments with a fixed pitch, such as the piano.   ▶ 10 / 8

VIBRATO

REPEATING MUSIC

We'll end with a look at some of the methods which have evolved over the centuries to help save time and space and to make music easier to read.

A great deal of music revolves around repetition. If music was always marked out in full you would find that huge segments were almost identical. Fortunately this isn't necessary – using a number of symbols it is possible to repeat individual notes, bars and even whole sections of music.

REPEATING NOTES

The stroke symbol is the standard musical shorthand for repeating individual notes or alternating patterns of notes. The positioning of a single stroke through any of kind of note is an instruction to play the same number of quavers that make up the value of that note. For example, the semibreve with a single stroke either above or below (see right) means that eight quavers of the same pitch are to be played.

As you can see, this is a far more economical way of notating music. The addition of a second stroke means that the reiteration must be in semiquavers (see bottom three examples on the right). The addition of

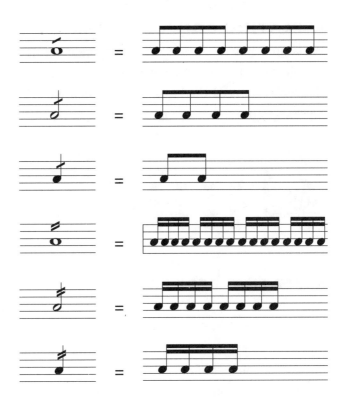

third and fourth strokes for demisemiquavers and hemidemisemiquavers are also possible.

The same principle can be used for alternating pairs of notes. In the example below, the semiquavers in the first bar can be reduced to the two alternating semibreves with double strokes in the second bar.

REPEATING WITHIN BARS

Bars and their components can be repeated by using a variety of "slash" symbols. These can also be used effectively in informal chord charts where only the names of the chords are written out.

One or more oblique slashes following a chord within a bar is an instruction to repeat that chord on as many beats on which there is a slash. The example below shows a C major chord repeated on each beat

of the first bar. In the second bar the chord is only shown once followed by three slashes – both bars will sound identical.

Grouped notes within the bar can also be repeated in this way. A single slash following a group of beamed quavers is an instruction to repeat that group – a double stroke ("//") is used to repeat a group of semiquavers; a triple stroke ("///") to repeat a group of demisemiquavers.

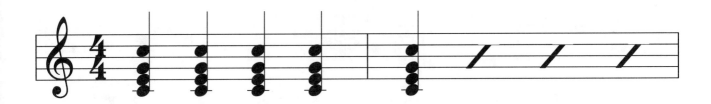

REPEATING COMPLETE BARS

An entire bar, or series of bars, can be repeated using a slash symbol with dots either side (✗). Whenever this symbol is used the 1st bar with notated music is repeated until further instruction.

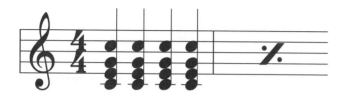

REPEATING REST BARS

A rest bar, as the name suggests, is a bar that consists of a single rest. Although it may seem a strange notion, if you listen to an orchestral work you will discover that not all of the musicians are playing all of the time. Indeed, some players who only have a small role in a piece of music will be silent for most of the time. Nevertheless, it is still crucial for these players to follow the score so that they know when their own parts have to be played.

In previous centuries, shorthand techniques evolved to aid this problem. A selection of multiple bar rest symbols were developed for gaps of between two and eight bars. Thereafter, the bar appeared with

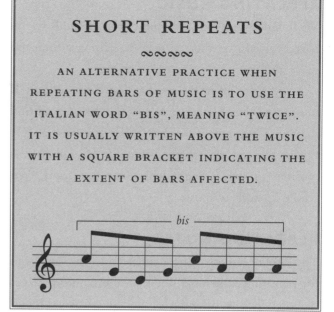

SHORT REPEATS

∞∞∞∞

AN ALTERNATIVE PRACTICE WHEN REPEATING BARS OF MUSIC IS TO USE THE ITALIAN WORD "BIS", MEANING "TWICE". IT IS USUALLY WRITTEN ABOVE THE MUSIC WITH A SQUARE BRACKET INDICATING THE EXTENT OF BARS AFFECTED.

a thick horizontal line and a number above. This told the player very literally how many bars of rest were ahead. Over the past century this practice has been adopted for all rests of two bars or more.

The example below shows an instruction that the player must rest for the next 32 bars.

REPEATING SECTIONS

You have already seen a simple example of a repeat sequence earlier in the course. This was by the positioning of a pair dots at the start and end of a double bar line to indicate that EVERYTHING within those bars has to be repeated. In practice, the issue of repeating long segments of music can be quite complex and it can be very easy to become confused.

Repeat bars are usually shown in pairs. The only exception is when the opening repeat is the start of the music. Look at the simplified example below and follow the sequence of events on the right.

- **1.** Play bars 1 and 2.
- **2.** The repeat sign at the end of bar 2 sends you back to the start of the piece.
- **3.** Repeat bars 1 and 2.
- **4.** This time you ignore the repeat sign at the end of bar 2 – you only react to it once otherwise you will never get beyond bar 2.
- **5.** Play bars 3 and 4.
- **6.** The repeat sign at the end of bar 4 instructs you to return to the previous "start repeat" sign, which is at the beginning of Bar 3.
- **7.** Repeat bars 3 and 4 and continue onward.

BAR 1   BAR 2   BAR 3   BAR 4

OTHER REPEAT INSTRUCTIONS

More complex reiterations are possible by using the instructions *Da Capo* and *Dal Segno*. *Da Capo* means "from the head". It is an instruction that the piece has to repeated from the start until the score indicates *fine* ("the end") or an alternative instruction. *Da Capo* is usually shown as "D.C." beneath the bar ending.

The *Dal Segno* symbol works in a similar fashion, literally meaning "from the sign". This is an instruction that the piece has to repeated from the sign 𝄋. Again, the music plays through until reaching *fine*.

ENDINGS

It is possible to give a repeated passage an alternative ending using the first- and second-time bar brackets. In this example, bars 1 to 4 are played to the repeat sign. Bars 1 to 3 are then replayed. The first-time bar bracket indicates that bar 4 is only played on the first cycle, therefore it is omitted, leaving the piece to end on bar 5. ▶ 10 / 9

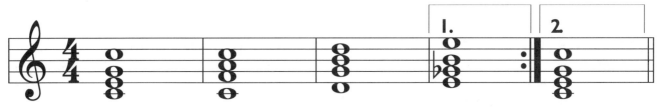

TEST 29

WORK OUT THE ORDER IN WHICH THE NINE BARS ARE PLAYED ACCORDING TO THE REPEAT SIGNS.

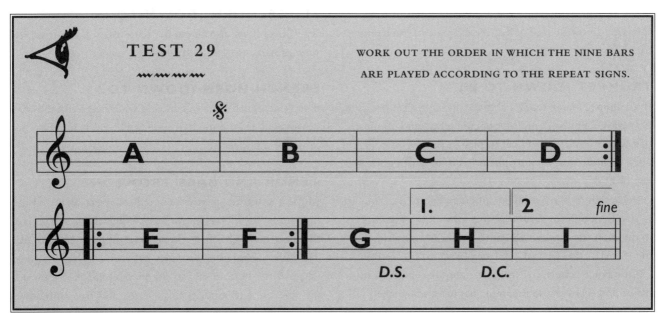

TIME OUT: SUMMARY OF LESSON 10

HERE IS A SUMMARY OF THE MAIN POINTS COVERED IN THIS LESSON.

- DYNAMIC MARKS
- STACCATO
- ACCIACCATURA AND APPOGIATURA

- TRILLS AND MORDENTS
- TREMOLO AND VIBRATO
- REPEAT SYMBOLS

APPENDIX A:

Instrumental Matters

The basic rules for learning how to read music can be related to any instrument. However, some have their own special needs when it comes to notation. Several brass and reed instruments, for example, are transposed so that the notes written on the staff are not the same as concert pitch. On the next four pages notated examples are shown as the instrumentalist sees them; the note ranges written beneath show true concert pitch.

BRASS INSTRUMENTS

Brass instruments can be notoriously difficult to notate because many members of the family are what is known as TRANSPOSING INSTRUMENTS. This means that the notes they play will appear at a different pitch to most of the other instruments. Look at the example of the trumpet to see how this works.

TRUMPET (DOWN TO B♭)

If a trumpet player reads and plays the note C, what you hear played will be B♭ in terms of concert pitch. This means that if you want the trumpet to play in the key of concert pitch C, music for the instrument has to be written for the key of D.

Although this may sound quite complex, the rule is relatively straightforward: whatever interval the instrument in question transposes by, the music must be transcribed by the SAME INTERVAL in the OPPOSITE DIRECTION. For example, the trumpet transposes DOWN by a major 2nd (C to B♭), so the music has to be transcribed UP by a major 2nd (C to D).

All of the staves shown on across the page reflect of the range of the instrument as read by the musician – the true concert pitch (if different) is marked beneath.

PICCOLO TRUMPET (UP TO D)

This is particularly high-pitched trumpet which transposes up by a major 2nd. Indeed, it is often referred to as the "D trumpet". Its range is identical to the trumpet, but its sound is very different, especially in the higher register where it creates a much purer tone.

CORNET (DOWN TO B♭)

The cornet is essentially a trumpet with conical rather than cylindrical tubing.

FLUGELHORN (DOWN TO B♭)

The flugel horn also obeys the same rules as the trumpet, though its range is slightly less.

FRENCH HORN (DOWN TO F)

The french horn has a remarkably wide range and thus can be notated over both bass and treble clefs. It transposes down by a perfect 5th.

TENOR AND BASS TROMBONE

Music for the tenor trombone (the correct term for the instrument most of us know as the trombone) is notated on the bass clef. The first three notes shown are PEDAL TONES, or drones – the notes between the highest pedal (B♭) and the bottom end of the playable range (E) are not possible on a trombone. Both tenor and bass trombones play at concert pitch.

TUBA

The tuba is the lowest-pitched brass instrument and hence music for the instrument is written on the bass clef. The notes below the lowest "F" can only be played as pedal tones. The small number "8" below the bottom note indicates that it is an octave lower than the notes defined by the bass clef.

There are a number of different types of tuba, but they generally play at concert pitch.

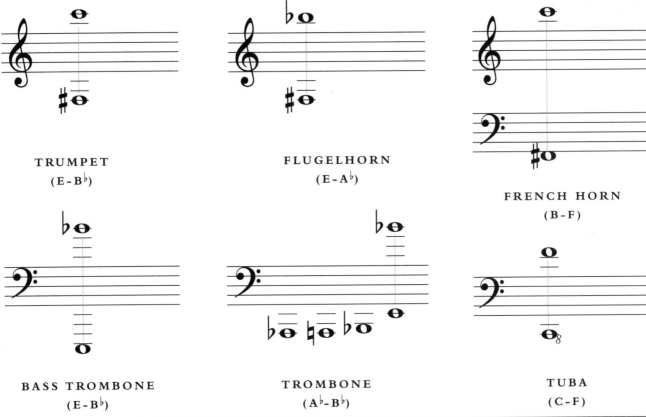

TRUMPET
(E - B♭)

FLUGELHORN
(E - A♭)

FRENCH HORN
(B - F)

BASS TROMBONE
(E - B♭)

TROMBONE
(A♭ - B♭)

TUBA
(C - F)

WIND INSTRUMENTS

Like their brass counterparts, several members of the wind family transpose.

ALTO FLUTE (DOWN TO G)

The regular "concert" flute plays at concert pitch. The bass flute transposes down by an octave. The alto flute, however, transposes down by a perfect 4th.

BASSOON

The bassoon is classified as a "double reed" instrument. This is because it does not have a conventional mouthpiece but two reeds tied together. Its treble equivalent, the oboe, also plays at concert pitch.

CLARINET (DOWN TO B♭)

There are a number of different types of clarinet, although the B♭ is the most common variety.

SAXOPHONE FAMILY (VARIOUS)

The four principle saxophone types have vastly different pitch ranges but all are transposed so that music written for ANY saxophone appears to be the same.

The complete range is as follows: the soprano saxophone transposes down to B♭; the alto, down to E♭; the tenor down to B♭ beyond the octave; and the baritone down to E♭ beyond the octave.

ALTO FLUTE
(G - G)

CLARINET
(G - F)

OBOE
(B♭ - G)

BASSOON
(B♭ - E♭)

SAXOPHONES
SOPRANO (A♭ - E♭)
ALTO (D♭ - D♭)
TENOR (A♭ - E♭)
BARITONE (D♭ - D♭)

THE STRING FAMILY

There are four instruments that make up the string family. They are the violin, viola, cello and double bass. The way in which each instrument is tuned is shown in brackets, with strings named from the lowest to the highest.

VIOLIN

(G – D – A – E)

The highest pitch instrument in the family, the violin has a practical range of G below middle C to the note E three-and-a-half octaves higher.

VIOLA

(C – G – D – A)

Similar in appearance to the violin, the slightly larger viola is lower in pitch. A quirk of written music for the viola is that it is some of its range is often written using an alto clef. The notes on the alto clef are F-A-C-E-G (lines) and G-B-D-F (spaces).

CELLO (VIOLONCELLO)

(C – G – D – A)

Music for the cello is sometimes written on the tenor clef, however in practice, most cellists are more familiar with the bass clef.

DOUBLE BASS

(E – A – D – G)

Parts written for the double bass are transposed up by an octave, thus the pitch range of E to G is written an octave higher. As most bass music is played in the lower register it becomes easier to read when raised onto the staff (most of

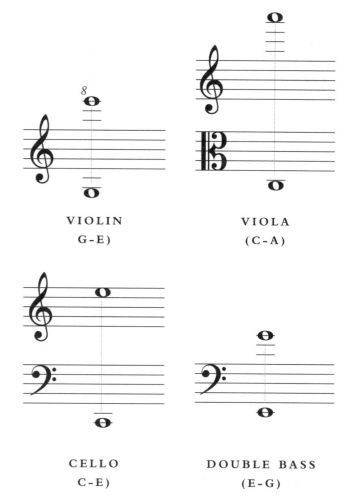

VIOLIN
G-E)

VIOLA
(C-A)

CELLO
C-E)

DOUBLE BASS
(E-G)

the notes would otherwise appear on ledger lines). This practice also holds true for bass guitars.

Notes higher than G are possible, but intonation, even among good players, can be poor in this register – in any case, in most orchestral settings, the cello would be more likely to take one these roles.

THE HUMAN VOICE

∞∞∞

SINCE THE 19TH CENTURY, SINGING VOICES HAVE BEEN CLASSIFIED ACCORDING TO FOUR BASIC TYPES: BASS AND TENOR FOR MALES; ALTO AND SOPRANO FOR FEMALES. THEIR APPROXIMATE PITCH RANGES ARE SHOWN BELOW. AS YOU CAN SEE, THERE IS CONSIDERABLE CROSSOVER BETWEEN EACH PAIR.

MOST NATURAL VOICES, IN FACT, FALL SOMEWHERE BETWEEN EACH RANGE. MOST MALE VOICES ARE BARITONE; MOST FEMALE VOICES MEZZO SOPRANO. OTHER TERMS ARE ALSO SOMETIMES HEARD: BASSO-PROFUNDO DESCRIBES AN EXCEPTIONALLY LOW MALE BASS VOICE. SIMILARLY, A MALE SINGING IN THE ALTO RANGE IS CALLED A COUNTER-TENOR. A FALSETTO IS A MALE SOPRANO.

BASS   TENOR   ALTO   SOPRANO

DRUMS AND PERCUSSION
~~~~

WRITTEN MUSIC FOR DRUMS AND THE PERCUSSION FAMILY DEPENDS ON THE PRECISE NATURE OF THE INSTRUMENTS THEMSELVES. MULTI-PITCHED INSTRUMENTS LIKE THE GLOCKENSPIEL AND XYLOPHONE USE STANDARD NOTATION, WRITTEN RESPECTIVELY ONE AND TWO OCTAVES LOWER. PITCHED PERCUSSION, SUCH AS THE TIMPANI (KETTLE DRUM) CAN BE WRITTEN ON THE BASS CLEF – THE CHARACTERISTIC CHANGES IN PITCH PRODUCED BY A FOOT PEDAL OR TUNING KEY ARE SHOWN AS REGULAR GLISSANDOS.

NOTATING A FULL RHYTHM PART FOR A STANDARD DRUM KIT PROVIDES CERTAIN COMPLICATIONS SINCE THIS MANNER OF PLAYING HAS LARGELY DEVELOPED OVER THE PAST CENTURY AND HAS ALMOST NO ROLE IN THE REGULAR CLASSICAL REPERTOIRE. MOST COMPOSERS IN THE POPULAR MUSIC IDIOMS LEAVE SUCH MATTERS TO THE DISCRETION OF THE PERFORMER, AT MOST PROVIDING GENERAL INSTRUCTIONS RELATING TO STYLE AND FEEL. EVEN IN THE MOST FORMAL JAZZ SETTINGS, WHERE ALL THE OTHER INSTRUMENTAL PARTS ARE CAREFULLY MAPPED OUT, IT IS STILL RARE FOR A DRUM PART TO BE NOTATED IN FULL.

NONETHELESS, IT IS POSSIBLE TO PROVIDE NOTATION FOR A FULL DRUM KIT USING A STAFF WITH A TIME SIGNATURE BUT NO CLEF. AS THE PITCH CREATED BY EACH COMPONENT OF THE KIT DOESN'T ALTER, THE LINES AND SPACES CAN BE USED TO SCORE DIFFERENT DRUM VOICES. STANDARD NOTATION IS USED TO PROVIDE NOTE VALUES. SOMETIMES CROSSED NOTE HEADS CAN BE USED TO MAKE THE PART EASIER TO READ. THE KEY TO THE INSTRUMENTS IS WRITTEN AT THE BEGINNING OF THE STAFF - IN THIS EXAMPLE THE BASS DRUM APPEARS ON THE BOTTOM LINE.

GUITAR
(E – A – D – G – B – E)

Parts written for the guitar are transposed up by an octave. To be technically correct, guitar music should be shown on a treble clef with a small "8" on its tail – this denotes that all the music written on this staff should be played an octave higher. In practice this instruction is often taken for granted and a regular treble clef is used.

Notice that the range shown on the right covers a full four octaves. The highest notes are only possible on certain types of electric guitar – those with a 24-fret (two-octave) fingerboard. The generally poor access to the higher register on the traditional Spanish guitar means that it is relatively unusual for classical guitarists to play beyond the 15th fret of the top string – this is the note G. It is, however, possible to create higher-pitched notes on lower fret positions by using harmonics.

It is also sometimes possible to play below the note E on the lowest string. "Altered tuning" – deviation from the standard tuning shown above – can be used to create a wide variety of different effects. However, if the lowest string is taken down further than a major 3rd it may well become too slack to provide a consistent tone. Alternatively, the development of the relatively rare seven-string guitar allows for a much fuller bass range, with the addition of a B string below the bottom E.

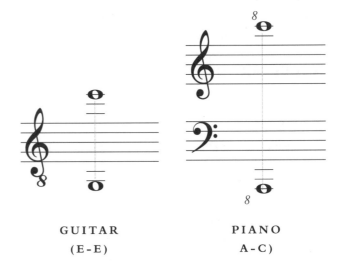

GUITAR
(E-E)

PIANO
A-C)

PIANO

Technically a percussion instrument (because each key is attached to a hammer that strikes against the strings), the piano comes in a wide variety of shapes and sizes, from the smallest of "uprights" to the largest of concert grands. A concert grand piano has one of of widest pitch ranges of any instrument, beginning with the note A – over three octaves below middle C – to the note C, three octaves above middle C. To notate music that covers this massive range, octave symbols must be added above the treble staff and below the bass staff.

APPENDIX B:

Dictionary of Terms

There are tens of thousands of musical terms that there is insufficient space to cover within the course. Here is a dictionary of some of the more common expressions you may come into contact with when reading a piece of music or discussing music theory. This list, which is by no means exhaustive, also acts as a handy reference if you need reminding of terms you have previously encountered.

ABSTOSSEN
See Staccato.

A CAPPELLA
Literally meaning "at the chapel", choral music sung without the accompaniment of a musical instrument.

ACCELERANDO
Becoming faster.

ACCENT
A dynamic playing effect that places an emphasis on specific notes of chords within a sequence, making them louder or creating rhythmic effects.

ACCIACCATURA
An ornamental effect sometimes called a "crushed note". The acciaccatura "prefixes" a regular note, but is shown in small type to indicate that its duration is not included in the value of the bar. In practice, it represents a very fast move between the two notes so that the acciaccatura is barely perceptible. It should be played on the beat of the principal note.

ACCOLADE
See Brace.

ACCIDENTAL
Symbols used in written music to raise or lower the pitch of a note by one or two semitones. A sharp (♯) raises the pitch by a semitone; a double sharp (𝄪) raises the pitch by two semitones; a flat (♭) lowers the pitch by a semitone; and the double flat (♭♭) lowers the pitch by two semitones. The effect of sharps and flats can be "switched off" with the use of a symbol known as a natural (♮).

ACCOMPANIMENT
Any form of musical backing. Usually applies to vocalists but can also be used to distinguish between primary and secondary musical roles.

ACCORDARE/ACCORDER
To tune.

ACOUSTIC(S)
A non-electric instrument; the science of the behaviour of sound – crucial to a musician's aural perception.

ACTION
The mechanism on a piano or organ that creates a sound when a key is played; the height of the strings above the frets on a guitar.

ADAGIO

Literally meaning "at ease", a slow tempo which is faster than andante but slower than largo. It's diminutive form is *adagietto*, which is slightly faster than *adagio*.

ADAGISSIMO

Extremely slow – slower than *adagio*.

ADDED NINTH CHORD

An interval of a 9th added above the root of a triad. Distinct from a ninth chord, which simply adds the 9th to a seventh chord.

ADDOLORATO

Performance mark literally meaning "pained" or "stricken".

AD LIBITUM

Instruction that the performer may freely interpret or improvise a passage. It may also mean that within a score a vocal or instrumental part may be omitted.

AOLIAN MODE

Modal scale starting on the 6th degree of the major scale.

AFFETUOSO

Direction that a piece should be performed tenderly; a term loosely connected to 17th-century Doctrine of Affections, a belief held by a group of composers that the function of music should be to arouse the passions of the listener, be it with love, hate or joy.

AGITATO

Performance direction literally meaning "agitated".

AIR

A tune – vocal or instrumental.

ALBERTI BASS

A bass figure made popular by the Italian composer Domenico Alberti (1709-1740) in which the notes of a triad were played in a 1st-5th-3rd-5th sequence. The most significant example is Mozart's "Piano Sonata in C Major (K.545)".

ALLA BREVE

Played with a minim beat – equates to a time signature of two-two.

ALLA MARCIA

An instruction to play in the style of a march.

ALLEGRO

Played at a fast tempo, literally meaning "quickly". Its diminutive form is *allegreto*, which is quite fast, but not as fast as *allegro*.

ALTERED CHORD

A chord in which one or more of the pitches has been altered by an accidental.

ALTO

A low female voice or a high male voice; the second highest vocal range, beneath soprano and above tenor.

ANDANTE

Medium-pace tempo played "at walking pace". *Andantino* usually means slightly faster than *andante*. *Molto andante* indicates that the tempo should be even slower.

ANIMANDO

Literally meaning "becoming animated" – an increase in tempo is also implied. Note, however, the related term *anima* has an ambiguous meaning which can be interpreted as an instruction to play with feeling or with spirit.

APPOGIATURA

A grace note or "leaning" note, distinct from the accacciatura, receiving half the value of the principle note. It can also be used to indicate pitch bends on stringed instruments.

WRITTEN   PLAYED

ARCHETTO/ARCO

The bow of a stringed instrument.

ARCHO/ARCHI

An instruction to resume playing with the bow after having played pizzicato.

ARIA

A self-contained piece of music for a single voice with instrumental accompaniment. Can also form a part of a larger work, such as an opera.

ARPEGGIO

The notes of a chord played in quick succession rather than simultaneously. Commonly notated using a wavy line. Also known as a "broken chord".

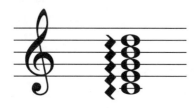

ARTICULATION

The attack with which single notes or chords are played and the length of time over which they are allowed to decay. Articulation symbols written on the staff can include the slur, which marks out phrases, and staccato which shortens the length of a note.

A TEMPO

Literally meaning "in time", an instruction to return to the original tempo after deviations.

ATONAL

Music composed with the deliberate suppression of the central tonic triad and use of diatonic harmony, allowing the twelve pitches of the chromatic scale to be used freely.

AUGMENTED

Interval created by raising a perfect or major interval by a semitone.

AUXILIARY NOTE

Used in counterpoint to describe a note which is a tone above or below a consonant note.

BACKBEAT

Term used in modern music to describe the rhythmic effect of a heavy snare drum beat on the second and fourth beats of a bar.

BAR

Sometimes referred to as a "measure", a unit of musical time in which the notes contained within total a fixed combined value defined by the time signature. Bars are separated by bar lines.

BARRE

Method of playing polyphonic stringed instruments such as the guitar by positioning the index finger across the strings enabling the player to hold down adjacent notes of a chord along the fingerboard.

BASS

The lowest part in a polyphonic composition; the lowest-pitched male voice; term used to describe the double bass or the bass guitar; a range of low frequencies that can be electronically filtered.

BEAT

A metrical pulse grouped together to form recurring patterns or rhythms.

BEL CANTO

A singing technique which emphasizes even tone throughout the vocal range – literally translates as "beautiful singing".

BIND

See Tie.

BIS

An instruction to repeat a short passage.

BITONALITY

The simultaneous use of two or more keys within a piece of music.

BRACE

Symbol used to join together staves that are to be played simultaneously. Piano music usually shows a treble staff and a bass staff played by the right and left hands respectively.

BRASS INSTRUMENTS

A family of tubular wind instruments which includes the trumpet, tuba and trombone.

BRAVURA, CON

An instruction that a composition or passage requires a virtuoso display by the performer.

BREATH MARKS

Symbol used to in vocal music to denote where breath should be taken. Usually shown by as "✳".

BREVE/BREVIS

The short note in mensural notation (the counterpart to the *longa* – long note) the modern-day equivalent of two semibreves.

BROKEN CHORD

See Arpeggio.

CADENCE

A musical phrase that creates the sense of rest or resolution at its end. The most commonly used cadence is the "perfect cadence".

CADENZA

An ornamental passage frequently performed over the penultimate notes or chord in a cadence. In most cases this cadence signals the end of the composition or movement and will resolve to the tonic.

CADENZATO

Rhythmic.

CALANDO

Getting softer – dying away.

CALMATO

Play in a calm, tranquil manner.

CANTARE SUPER LIBRUM

Vocal improvisation on an existing melody.

CAPO/CAPOTASTO

Mechanical bar fitted to a fretted stringed instrument for the purposes of transposition.

CAPRICCIOSO

Instruction that a piece should be played capricioulsy or at the player's whim.

CASTRATO

A male singer castrated as a child in order to preserve his alto or soprano vocal range. Also known as "eviratos", castratos were widely used in operatic music during the 17th and 18th centuries.

CELERE/CELEREMENTE

Instruction to play swiftly.

CHAMBER MUSIC

Compositions created to be performed for a small ensemble, most notably a string quartet.

CHANSON

The French word for "song". The term has a wide variety of ambiguous uses in music.

CHORAL MUSIC

Music performed by a choir or chorus with each individual part sung by more than one vocalist.

CHORD

The sound of three or more notes of different pitch played simultaneously. A three-note chord is known as a triad.

CHROMATIC

A scale that includes all twelve pitches with each degree separated by a semitone.

CIRCLE OF FIFTHS

Closed circle of all twelve pitches arranged at intervals of a perfect 5th. First devised by Johann David Heinechen in the 18th century.

CLEF

Symbol placed at the beginning of a staff or bar line that determines the pitches of the notes and lines on the staff that follow. Three types are commonly used: the G or treble clef; the F or bass clef; and the C clef. The C clef as shown is termed the alto clef and when centred on the fourth line it becomes the tenor clef.

TREBLE   BASS   ALTO

CLOSE HARMONY

Term to describe the three uppermost voices singing in close triads in four-part harmony,

CODA

The concluding passage of a piece of music.

COMMON CHORD

A major triad.

COMMON TIME

Music written with a time signature of four-four or two-two. Indicated by the clef symbols "**C**" (four-four) and "**₵**" (two-two).

COMODO

Instruction to play at a comfortable speed.

COMPOUND INTERVAL

An interval of greater than an octave.

CONCERT PITCH

The set of reference tones to which all non-transposing instruments must be tuned. A common scientific definition is that the note "A" below "middle C" is measured as having a frequency of 440 cycles/second.

CONCORD

The description given to intervals that are deemed to be consonant. Specifically, they are the intervals between the root note (1st) and the 3rd, 4th, 5th, 6th and 8th notes respectively.

CONTRALTO

The lowest female voice.

COUNTERMELODY

A subordinate melody that accompanies a main melody.

COUNTERPOINT

Two or more lines of melody played at the same time.

COUNTERTENOR

A male alto.

CRESCENDO

A performance mark that indicates a gradual increase in loudness. The opposite of *diminuendo* or *decrescendo*.

CROTCHET

A note worth one beat within a bar of four-four time.

DA CAPO

Literally meaning "from the head", *da capo* is an instruction that the performer must return to the beginning of the piece and conclude at the double bar marked *fine*, or an alternative repeat sign such as *al segno* or "𝄋". The term is usually abbreviated as **D.C.**.

DAL SEGNO

Literally meaning "from the sign", an instruction that the performer must repeat a sequence from a point marked by the sign "𝄋". Abbreviated as **D.S.**.

DAMP

To cause the vibrations of a string to stop ringing either by muting with the right hand or the immediate loosening of the fingers of the left hand.

DECISO/DECISAMENTE

Instruction to play decisively with resolve.

DECRESCENDO

See *Crescendo* and *Diminuendo*.

DELICATO

Instruction to play delicately.

DEMISEMIQUAVER

A note worth an eighth of a beat within a four-four bar. Termed a thirty-second note in the US. See Notes.

DIABOLUS IN MUSICA

The "devil in music"; the name given in the 17th century to the "tritone" – an interval of three whole tones. Deemed dissonant, the use of the interval was prohibited by various music theorists of the time.

DIATONIC

The seven-note major and minor scale system.

DIMINISHED

An interval created by lowering a perfect or minor interval by a semitone; also a term applied both to a minor chord with a lowered 5th note and a chord that comprises minor 3rd intervals.

DIMINUENDO

A performance mark that indicates a gradual decrease in loudness. The opposite of *crescendo*. Sometimes referred to as *decrescendo*.

DISCORD

The description given to note intervals that are deemed to be dissonant in character. Specifically this refers to the intervals between the root note (1st) and the 2nd and 7th notes respectively.

DOMINANT

The 5th degree of a major or minor scale. The triad built on this degree is the dominant triad; the seventh built on this degree is the dominant seventh.

DOPPIO MOVIMENTO

An instruction to perform a passage at double the tempo.

DORIAN MODE

The modal scale built from the 2nd degree of the major scale.

DOTTED NOTES

A dot positioned after any type of note which increases its value by half. A second dot can be added to increase the value by a quarter; a third dot added increases the value by an eighth.

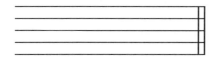

DOTTED RESTS

A dot positioned after a rest to increase its value by half. Most commonly found in compound time.

DOUBLE

To perform the same set of notes on two similar or different instruments. The two parts can be played at the same pitch or an interval of an octave.

DOUBLE BAR

Two vertical lines drawn through the staff to indicate the end of a piece of music or a movement.

DOUBLE FLAT

See Accidentals.

DOUBLE SHARP

See Accidentals.

DUET

A composition for two performers.

DUOLO/DOLORE

Instruction to play with sorrow or grief.

DYNAMIC MARKS

Terms, symbols and abbreviations used to indicate different levels of volume or a transition from one level to another.

EMBOUCHURE

The correct positioning of the lips and mouth for players of wind instruments.

EMPFINDUNG, MIT

German-language term – an instruction to perform with feeling or emotion.

ENHARMONIC

A set of different names that may be applied to the same pitches. For example, the notes C♯ and D♭ are deemed to be enharmonic equivalents.

ESPRESSIVO

Instruction to play expressively.

EXPRESSION MARKS

Words or symbols written on a score to guide the player on matters other than pitch or rhythm – dynamics, articulation and tempo, for example.

FACILE/FACILMENTE

Play easily.

FALSETTO

A male voice that sings in the female soprano range.

FERMATA

Pause. A symbol placed above or below a note or rest that indicates that it should be held for longer than its natural duration. Before the 20th century it was traditionally known as a corona.

FLAT

See Accidentals.

FLEBILE

Plaintive or mournful.

FORTE/FORTISSIMO/FORTISSISSIMO

A set of instructions for the performer to play louder, of which *forte* is the quietest and *fortissimo* the loudest. The terms are abbreviated using a stylized script as ***f***, ***ff*** and ***fff*** respectively.

FORTE-PIANO

An instruction to play loud then soft. Shown in a stylized script as *pf*.

FORZA/FORZANDO

Instructions to play with strength or force.

FRET

A strip of metal placed across the fingerboard of some stringed instruments, such as the guitar, lute or mandolin, that allows the strings to be held down on the fingerboard at a predetermined pitch.

FUGUE

Form of composition in which a theme, once established by one voice is taken up by another. The initial voice is then used to provide a counterpoint accompaniment. This process continues irrespective of the number of voices used.

GATHERING NOTE

The note given by an organist to provide a choir with a reference tone for the singing of hymns.

GENERALPAUSE

German word that literally means "general pause". A rest for all players within an orchestral score. Usually shown on the staff as G.P.

GLISSANDO

A continuous sliding movement between two different pitches. On a piano keyboard the effect can be produced by running the nails of a finger along the black or white notes, creating a very fast scale of discretely pitched notes. On other instruments this effect creates a continuous change in pitch which is sometimes referred to as PORTAMENTO. The effect is shown on written music by joining the upper and lower notes with a line. A lower-case letter "s" may also be shown above the line.

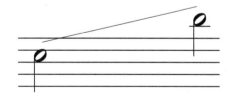

GRACE NOTE

See Appogiatura.

GRAZIOSO

Instruction to play with grace.

GREGORIAN CHANT

Also known as plainsong, the predominant liturgical chant used during the middle ages.

HALF STEP

US term that describes a semitone interval.

HARMONIC

A bell-like effect created on stringed instruments by the positioning of the finger over specific points along the length of the string. Indicated by a small open circle above the note or with a diamond-headed note.

HARMONY

The effect of a set of notes played simultaneously, and how these intervals and chords sound in relation to each other.

HEMIDEMISEMIQUAVER

A note worth a sixteenth of a beat within a bar of four-four time. Termed a sixty-fourth note in the US. See Notes.

HEXACHORD

A simultaneous collection of six pitches.

IMPERFECT CADENCE

A cadence which moves from the tonic to the dominant – usually a phrase in the middle of a piece of music.

IMPROVISATION

At one extreme, the creation of an original work during the course of a performance. In the classical tradition improvisation tends to be limited to allowing the performer a greater degree of flexibility in ornamentation and other discretionary areas.

INTERRUPTED CADENCE

A cadence which moves from the dominant to any chord other than the tonic.

INTERVAL

The relationship between two different pitches numbered in terms of the degrees of the diatonic scale system.

INTONATION

The degree to which tuning and pitching is accurate among the musicians in an ensemble.

INVERSION

The order of notes in a chord from the lowest pitch. If the root is the lowest note, the chord is said to be in the root position. If the 3rd note is the lowest, the chord is a first inversion; if the 5th note is the lowest, it is a second inversion; if a 7th note has the lowest pitch, the chord is called a third inversion.

IONIAN MODE

A modal scale from which the diatonic major scale was originally derived.

JOYEUX

Instruction that a piece of music should be played joyfully.

KEY

The reference pitch for a diatonic scale.

KEYNOTE

An alternative name for the 1st degree of a diatonic scale.

KEY SIGNATURE

An arrangement of sharps and flats on the staff that defines the key.

LAMENTOSO/LAMENTABILE

An instruction for the performer to play a piece of music with a mood of sadness.

LARGO

Slow or stately

LONGA

In mensural notation, the long or *maxima* note.

LEADING NOTE

The 7th degree of the diatonic major scale.

LEDGER LINE

A short line that allows notes to be transcribed outside of the range of the five-line staff.

LEGATO

An instruction to play a sequence of notes as smoothly as possible with no separation between successive notes. Often indicated within the boundaries of a slur but also sometimes abbreviated as *Leg*.

LEGNO

Instruction to bowed string players to strike the strings with the wood of the bow rather than the hair.

LENTO

Instruction to play extremely slowly.

L.H.

Left hand.

LIBRETTO

The text for an opera.

LICENZA

Played freely with regard to tempo or rhythm.

LIGADO

On stringed instruments such as the guitar, the effect of bringing one of the fretting fingers down onto a vibrating string to create a note of a higher pitch. The opposite principle can also be used by bringing the finger away from the vibrating string to play a note of lower pitch. These terms are commonly known as "hammering-on" and "pulling off".

LOCO

Instruction to return to original pitch having having been instructed to play at an alternative pitch, usually an interval of an octave. Abbreviated as *loc*.

LOCRIAN MODE

Modal scale which starts on the 7th degree of the major scale.

LUGUBRE

To play mournfully.

LUNGA

Prolonged pause or period of rest.

LYDIAN MODE

Mode starting on the 4th degree of the major scale.

MAESTOSO

To play majestically.

MANCANDO

Instruction that the music should create the illusion of fading away. Abbreviated as *Manc*.

MARZIALE

Instruction to play in a military style.

M.D.

Mano destra, Main droit, right hand.

MEASURE
Alternative name for a bar.

MEDIANT
The 3rd degree of the major scale.

MELODY
A pattern of single notes that form a coherent sequence. Often simply described as a tune.

MENSURAL NOTATION
System of musical notation used between the 13th and 16th centuries, generally credited to Franco of Cologne (fl. ca. 1250). The principle note values were the *maxima*, *longa*, *brevis* and *semibrevis* (shown from left to right).

METER
See Tempo.

METRONOME
Mechanical device used to denote the tempo of a piece of music in beats per minute. Often known as "Maelzel's Metronome" after the man who patented the idea. The letters "MM" followed by a note-type and value are often used on printed music to specify the tempo.

M.G.
Main gauche, left hand.

MICROTONE
A measurable interval smaller than a semitone. Its use in Western musical forms is largely esoteric.

MIDDLE C
The centre note on a piano keyboard which is also an important reference tone for other orchestral instruments. It is notated on a ledger line below a staff anchored by a treble clef.

MIXOLYDIAN MODE
The mode starting on the 5th degree of the major scale.

MODE
A series of fixed scales that were predominant during the middle ages. The modern-day diatonic system of major and minor scales evolved from their existence. The seven modes that can be built from the major scale are Ionian (I), Dorian (II), Phrygian (III), Lydian (IV), Mixolydian (V), Aeolian (VI) and Locrian (VII).

MODERATO
Instruction to play at a moderate speed.

MODULATION
Movement from one key to another within a section of piece of music.

MONODY
Music consisting of a single melodic line.

MONOPHONY
Music that comprises a single line.

MORDENT
An ornamental instruction to play a single note as a "trill" with an adjacent note. An upper mordent (left) alternates with the note a semitone higher; the lower mordent (right) is played with the a semitone lower.

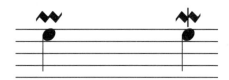

MOVEMENT
Any self contained segment of a larger work such as a symphony or concerto.

M.S.
Mano sinistra, left hand.

MUTE
A device or technique for reducing the volume on a musical instrument. On brass instruments the mute is a conical block that when placed in the bell reduces volume and alters the tone. The equivalent effect on the piano is the use of the damper pedal.

NATURAL
See Accidentals.

NEUME

Symbols used in the notation of plainsong between the 9th and 12th centuries.

NOTES

Symbols used in written music to indicate the pitch and duration of a sound. They are (shown from left to right): semibreve, minim, crotchet, quaver, semiquaver, demisemi-quaver, hemidemisemiquaver. In the United States an alternative series of names is used based around fractional values: whole note, half note, quarter note, eighth note, sixteenth note, thirty-second note and sixty-fourth note.

NOUVO

New.

OBBLIGATO

Literally meaning "obligatory", a term used to describe an accompanying secondary melody which is nonetheless extremely important and should not be omitted under any circumstances.

OCTAVE

An interval whose pitches have the same note name but the frequency of the lower note is half that of the upper note. Abbreviated as Ott., 8va or 8ve. When these marks are written above a staff, the notes should be played an octave higher in pitch; when written below the staff they should be played an octave lower.

OCTET

Chamber music written for eight musicians.

ONE-LINE

Any octave interval from middle C or from the notes within the octave starting with middle C.

OPUS

An non-specific term that refers to a musical composition. It is frequently used in designating a catalogue number to a composer's work. Usually abbreviated as *op*.

ORNAMENTATION

The alteration of a piece of music to make it sound more effective or beautiful. Usually through the addition of notes or dynamic changes.

OSSIA

A term used to indicate an alternative version of a passage – usually one which is easier to play.

OSTINATO

A short pattern that is repeated throughout a piece of music.

OTTAVA

Italian word for octave. See Octave.

OTTAVA BASSA/OTTAVA ALTA

Octave lower; octave higher.

OVERTURE

An orchestral composition that acts as an introduction to an extended work.

PARLATO/PARLANDO

Instruction to sing in a spoken style. Most commonly used in comic opera situations.

PASSING CHORD/NOTE

A chord or note whose function is clearly subordinate to the two on either side. It is, in effect, a kind of harmonic intermediary.

PAUSE

See Fermata.

PEDAL TONE

A bass note that sustains beneath any shifting harmonic structure. A typical example would be the bass "drone" produced by bagpipes.

PELOG

An Indonesian tuning used in gamelan music.

PENTACHORD

A chord comprising five different pitches.

PENTATONIC

A set of scales based around five notes. Among the oldest of scalar systems, pentatonic variants are used in musical culture all over the world. The minor pentatonic "blues scale" is commonly used in Jazz, R&B and rock music.

PERDENDOSI

Performance instruction to create the effect of the music fading away.

PERFECT CADENCE

A cadence that resolves from the dominant (V) to the tonic (I). The most commonly used form a cadence with which a piece of music is concluded.

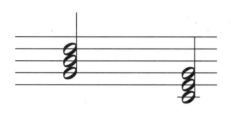

DOMINANT (V)   TONIC (I)

PERFORMANCE MARKS

Words or symbols written on a score to indicate aspects of performance not covered purely by pitches on the staff.

PHRASE

A self-contained musical sentence that can be viewed as a coherent and identifiable "whole" within the context of composition. Usually no more than a few bars in length, phrases are identified in written music within a slur.

PHRYGIAN MODE

The mode which is built from the 3rd degree of the diatonic major scale.

PIANO/PIANISSIMO/PIANISSISSIMO

Instructions for the performer to play softer, of which *pianississimo* is the quietest. Shown in a stylized script as ***p***, ***pp*** and ***ppp*** respectively.

PIANOFORTE

The technically correct name of the piano; also a performance instruction to play loud and then soft immediately afterwards. Usually shown on the score in a stylized script as ***pf***.

PIMA

The Spanish names given to the fingers of the right hand in classical guitar: "P" (*pulgar*) is the thumb; "I" (*indicio*) is the 1st/index finger; "M" (*medio*) is the 2nd finger; and "A" (*anular*) is the 3rd finger.

PITCH

The frequency of a note in terms of the number of times it vibrates each second.

PIZZICATO

In music written for strings, an instruction to pluck the notes with the fingers rather than play with a bow. Usually abbreviated as *pizz*.

PLAGAL CADENCE

A cadence that resolves from the subdominant (IV) to the tonic (I).

SUBDOMINANT (IV)   TONIC (I)

PLECTRUM

A device usually made from plastic, horn, tortoiseshell or ivory for plucking stringed instruments such as the guitar, mandolin or banjo. The term "pick" is also used.

POCO

Literally meaning "little". Derivatives include *poco a poco* ("little by little"), *fra poco* ("shortly"), *pochetto* or *pochettino* ("very little") and *pochimssimo* ("extremely little").

POLYCHORD

A chord which is made up of two different chords.

POLYPHONY

Music that combines two or more different lines.

PORTAMENTO

See Glissando.

PRALLTRILLER

Alternative name for the upper mordant.

PRELUDE

A self-contained composition whose function is both to attract the attention of the listener and to establish the pitch, key or mood of the music that follows immediately afterwards.

PRESTO

An instruction to play very fast – faster than *allegro*.

PRIMARY TRIADS

Term describing the three triads built from the tonic, subdominant and dominant degrees of a diatonic scale.

PRIMA/PRIMO

The Italian word that translates literally as "first"; used in conjunction with other performance marks such as *prima volta* ("first time") or *primo tempo* ("first tempo) – an instruction to revert to playing the tempo at which the composition began.

PUNTEADO

Technique by which the strings of a guitar are plucked rather than strummed.

QUARTER TONE

An interval whose value is half a semitone.

QUARTET

A composition written for four performers; the name given to an ensemble of four musicians.

QUAVER

A note with a value of half a crotchet. See Notes.

QUINTET

A composition written for five performers; the name given to an ensemble of five musicians.

QUINTUPLET

A group of five notes played in the time of four.

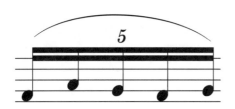

RAGA

A mode used in the music of Northern India.

RASGUEADO

A method of strumming used by Flamenco guitarists.

REED

A family of instruments that incorporate a reed fitted in the mouthpiece (or reeds tied together) to create their sound. The group includes the clarinet, saxophone, bassoon and oboe. The latter two are "double-reed" instruments.

REFRAIN

A segment from within a piece of music which is repeated periodically throughout. The chorus from within a pop song is a typical example.

REGISTER

The tonal range of a voice or instrument.

RELATIVE MAJOR/RELATIVE MINOR

The relationship between major and natural minor scales: the pitch of the notes and chords built on any major scale are the same as those on a natural minor scale built from the 6th degree of the major scale.

REPEAT/REITERATE

An instruction to reiterate a piece of music within the bars specified by repeat symbols.

REPRISE

The repetition of a sequence or theme.

RESOLUTION

A movement from a dissonant note to a consonant note.

REST

A symbol placed on the staff to indicate a period in which no notes are played. Each of the different note-types has an equivalent rest. They are (from left to right): semibreve, minim, crotchet, quaver, semiquaver, demisemiquaver, hemidemisemiquaver.

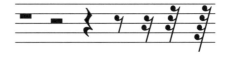

RESTRINGENDO

Literally meaning "becoming faster".

RETENU

Instruction to hold back and play more slowly.

R.H.

Instruction found in keyboard music to play a part with the right hand.

RHYTHM

A pattern or movement in time of notes and accents.

RIGOROSO

Strict.

RINFORZANDO

Instruction to suddenly accent notes.

RISOLUTO

Instruction to play boldly with energy.

RITARDANDO

Instruction to play gradually slower.

RITENUTO

An instruction to make a sudden reduction in tempo.

RUBATO, TEMPO

Literally meaning "stolen time". An instruction that allows the performer to ignore the prevailing tempo and speed up or slow down according to his or her own preference.

SCALE

A collection of notes laid out in a predefined sequence from the lowest pitch to the highest pitch.

C MAJOR SCALE

SCALE DEGREES

The position of each note within a scale. Can be shown numerically using Arabic or Roman numerals. Each degree can also be named: tonic (I); supertonic (II); mediant (III); subdominant (IV); dominant (V); submediant (VI); and leading note (VII).

SCHERZO/SCHERZANDO

Literally meaning "joke", an instruction to perform a piece of music playfully. There is also an implication of a fast tempo.

SCORE

The notation of an entire piece of music for an ensemble written out so that the simultaneous parts are aligned in a vertical manner.

SEGNO

Literally meaning "sign". The symbol ("𝄋") is used to mark the beginning or end of a repeated section. The sign must be paired with either a *dal segno* instruction, which means "from the sign", or an *al segno* instruction (meaning "to the sign").

SEGUE

A term indicating that the next piece of music follows immediately with no interruption.

SEMIQUAVER

A note whose value is half that of a quaver. See Notes.

SEMITONE

The interval between two adjacent pitches representing one twelfth of an octave. The smallest interval used in the vast majority of music in the western world. Termed a "half step" in the US.

SEMPRE

Literally meaning "always".

SEQUENCE

The repetition of a musical phrase at gradually increasing or decreasing intervals.

SEPTUPLET

A group of seven notes usually to be played in the time of four or six.

SEXTET

A composition written for six performers; the name given to an ensemble of six musicians.

SEXTUPLET

A group of six notes usually to be played in the time of four.

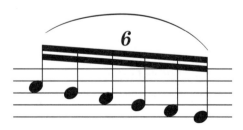

SFORZATO/SZFORZANDO

Literally meaning "forced" but usually interpreted as an instruction to play loud. Abbreviated as *sfz*.

SHARP

See Accidentals.

SIMILE

An instruction to continue playing as already marked; literally means "like".

SLIDE

See Glissando.

SOL-FA

A system of single-syllable abbreviations for the degrees of a scale: Do-Re-Me-Fa-Sol-La-Ti-Do.

SOPRANO

The highest pitched general vocal range.

SORDINO

Mute.

SPACE

The gap between the lines of a staff.

SPICCATO

A technique used by string players where the bow is bounced off the strings.

STACCATO

Literally meaning "detached", staccato notes or chords are dramatically reduced in length creating a "stabbing" effect. Usually shown in notation by a dot or an arrow head above or below the note.

STAFF

A group of horizontal parallel lines and spaces on which notes are placed to define their pitch. Sometimes also called a "stave" in the singular, but always "staves" in the plural.

STEM

The vertical line attached to the head of the note. The value of the note can be progressively halved by adding a tail (or flag) to the tip of the stem.

STEP

See Tone.

STRETTO

An instruction to quicken the tempo; overlapping elements in a fugue.

SUBDOMINANT

The 4th degree of a major scale.

SUBMEDIANT

The 6th degree of a major scale. Sometimes also called the superdominant.

SUPERTONIC

The 2nd degree of the major scale.

SYMPHONY

A work for orchestra which is made up from a series of independent movements.

SYNCOPATION

A rhythm that runs against the prevailing meter or pulse, emphasizing the off-beats.

TABLATURE

A type of diagramatic notation used for fretted instruments that illustrates the positions of notes on the frets and strings. At its simplest, tablature describes just the fingering. More complex versions that incorporate note values are also possible.

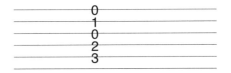

C MAJOR GUITAR CHORD
(FRET POSITIONS ON THE SIX STRINGS)

TEMPO

The speed at which the music is performed, usually measured in beats per second for a specific note type; see also Metronome.

TENEREZZA/TERAMENTE

Instruction to play tenderly.

TENOR

The vocal range directly above bass; the highest natural range for male vocalists.

TENUTO

An instruction that a note or chord should be held for at least its full duration, in some cases creating the effect of delaying the note that follows. The opposite to *staccato*.

TIE

A curved line joining two notes of the same pitch which indicates that the value of the second note must be added to the value of the first, and that the second note itself is NOT played. Mostly used to sustain notes across bar lines. Also known as "binds".

TIME SIGNATURE

The numerical symbols positioned at the beginning of a staff to indicate its meter. The upper number indicates the number of beats in the bar; the lower number shows the type of note that make up those beats.

TONALITY

The relationship of tones organized within a scale to a defined tonal centre. Music which can be described as tonal has an identifiable key.

TONE

An interval of a major 2nd (two semitones), known in the US as a "step"; a description of the colour or quality of a sound.

TONIC

The 1st degree of a scale.

TOSTO

Instruction to play swiftly or rapidly.

TRANQUILLO

An instruction to play in calm manner.

TRANSPOSITION

A piece of music rewritten at a different pitch to the original. Usually defined in terms of the difference in interval between the two.

TREMOLO

An ornamental effect based around the fast repetition of a single note. For bowed string players this is often created by the rapid up-and-down motion of the bow; the term is also sometimes used to describe the vibrato effect used by string players created by the rapid "rolling" of the left hand.

TRIAD

A chord made up of three notes separated by intervals of a 3rd. There are four different forms (from left to right): major; minor; diminished and augmented.

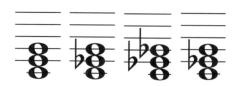

TRILL

A rapid alteration of two notes over a distance of a tone or semitone.

TRISTE/TRISTAMENTE

An instruction for the performer to play with a mood of sadness.

TRITONE

See Diabolus in Musica.

TRONCA

Cut off; accented.

TROPPO, NON

Literally meaning "not too much".

TRIPLET

A group of three notes played in the time of two.

TUNE

A melody; adjusting an instrument to concert pitch.

TURN

An ornamentation in which a marked note is played as fast succession of notes either side of its pitch.

TUTTI

Literally meaning "all", an instruction in a score that relates to everyone, not just the soloist.

UNISON

An interval of the same pitch.

VIBRATO

A slight fluctuation in pitch, not great enough to be defined as an interval.

VIVACE

An instruction to play in a lively or brisk manner.

VOLANTE

Literally meaning "flying", an instruction to play fast.

VOLTI SUBITO (V.S.)

Instruction to turn the sheet of music quickly.

WHOLE-TONE SCALE

Six-note scale comprising major 2nd intervals. Also known as an "augmented scale".

WOLF NOTE

A note on any type of acoustic instrument that is markedly different in tone or quality to the others, resulting from the acoustic properties of the instrument.

FOREIGN EQUIVALENTS
∞∞∞∞

THE TABLE BELOW SHOWS THE NOTE NAMES AND OTHER MUSICAL TERMS IN THE MAJOR MUSICAL LANGUAGES.

ENGLISH	FRENCH	GERMAN	ITALIAN
A	LA	A	LA
A SHARP	LA DIÉSE	AIS	LA DIESIS
A FLAT	LA BÉMOL	AES	LA BEMOLLE
B	SI	H	SI
B SHARP	SI DIÉSE	HIS	SI DIESIS
B FLAT	SI BÉMOL	B	SI BEMOLLE
C	UUT	C	DO
C SHARP	UT DIÉSE	CIS	DO DIESIS
C FLAT	UT BÉMOL	CES	DO BEMOLLE
D	RÉ	D	RE
D SHARP	RÉ DIÉSE	DIS	RE DIESIS
D FLAT	RÉ BÉMOL	D	RE BEMOLLE
E	MI	E	MI
E SHARP	MI DIÉSE	EIS	MI DIESIS
E FLAT	MI BÉMOL	EES	MI BEMOLLE
F	FA	F	FA
F SHARP	FA DIÉSE	FIS	FA DIESIS
F FLAT	FA BÉMOL	FES	FA BEMOLLE
G	SOL	G	SOL
G SHARP	SOL DIÉSE	GIS	SOL DIESIS
G FLAT	SOL BÉMOL	GES	SOL BEMOLLE
MAJOR	MAJEUR	DUR	MAGGORE
MINOR	MINEUR	MOLL	MINORE
SHARP	DIÉSE	KREUTZ	DIESIS
DOUBLE SHARP	DOUBLE DIÉSE	DOPPELKREUTZ	DOPPIO DIESIS
FLAT	BÉMOL	BE	BEMOLLE
DOUBLE FLAT	DOUBLE BÉMOL	DOPPEL-BE	DOPPIO-BEMOLLE
NATURAL	BÉCARRE	AUFLÔSUNGS-ZEICHEN	BEQUADRO
SEMIBREVE (US - WHOLE NOTE)	RONDE	GANZE	SEMIBREVE
MINIM (US - HALF NOTE)	BLANCHE	HALBE	BIANCA
CROTCHET (US - QUARTER NOTE)	NOIRE	VIERTEL	NERA
QUAVER (US - EIGHTH NOTE)	CROCHE	ACHTEL	CROMA
SEMIQUAVER (US - SIXTEENTH NOTE)	DOUBLE-CROCHE	SECHTZEHNTEL	SEMICROMA
DEMISEMIQUAVER (US - THIRTY-SECOND NOTE)	TRIPLE-CROCHE	ZWEIUND-DREISSIGSTEL	SEMIBISCROMA

Answers

Here are the answers to the 29 tests that you should have performed throughout the ten lessons of this course. Some are a matter of comparing your responses with the sounds of the CD – these are marked clearly. Elsewhere, if you get any of the answers wrong, go back to the relevant page in the book and ensure that you understand WHY your answer was wrong, and WHY the answer shown here is correct.

TEST 1 (PAGE 13)

1. A.
2. B.
3. A.
4. D.
5. B.
6. D.
7. C.
8. A.

TEST 2 (PAGE 15)

Exercise 1	C, A, G, E, F B, E, F.
Exercise 2	C, G, B, D D, F, A, G.
Exercise 3	F, B, A, G, C, G, C, D.
Exercise 4	F, E, D, G, B, C, D, E.
Exercise 5	G, D, G, C, G, D, C, B.

TEST 3 (PAGE 17)

Exercise 1	F, D, A, C, G, B, A, D.
Exercise 2	E, F, D, A, G, E, C, G.

TEST 4 (PAGE 20)

Exercise 1	C♯, F♯, E♭, F♯, F (F natural), E♭, G♯, F♯.
Exercise 2	B♭, F♯, D♭, C♯, G♯, F♯, B♭, B.
Exercise 3	C♯, G♯, D♭, G♯, G, B♭, C, A♯.
Exercise 4	C, B, C♯, D, B♭, E♭, F, G.
Exercise 5	F♯, C♯, G♯, C♯, E, A, G, G♯.

TEST 5 (PAGE 21)

Exercise 1	Note 3 (E) – it is F on the CD.
Exercise 2	Note 2 (D) – it repeats C on the CD.
Exercise 3	Note 4 (E) – it plays D on the CD.
Exercise 4	Note 1 (C) – it plays D on the CD.
Exercise 5	Note 4 (C) – it plays E on the CD.
Exercise 6	Note 2 (C) – it plays B on the CD.

TEST 6 (PAGE 27)

Check your answers against CD tracks 2/10, 2/11, 2/12, 2/13 and 2/14.

TEST 7 (PAGE 30)

Check your answers against CD tracks 2/18, 2/19 and 2/20.

TEST 8 (PAGE 32)

Exercise 1	Refer to CD track 2/22.
Notes:	C, F, E, D, E, C, G, F, F♯, F.
Exercise 2	Refer to CD track 2/23.
Notes:	C, B, A, G, C, C, D, D, G, F.
Exercise 3	Refer to CD track 2/24.
Notes:	B, A, G, A, B, D, C, B, A.
Exercise 4	Refer to CD track 2/25.
Notes:	C, G, A, F, C, A, F, C, D, F, E, G, F.
Exercise 5	Refer to CD track 2/26.
Notes:	C, E, F, G, G, A, F, D, F, G, A, B.

TEST 9 (PAGE 33)

Staff C matches track 2/27 on the CD.

TEST 10 (PAGE 33)

As the time signature is four-four, each bar should total four beats. In fact, both bars total more than this figure – bar one has a half beat too many and bar two has two beats too many.

One satisfactory solution would be simply to change the value of the crotchet rest (one beat) in bar one to a semi-quaver rest (half a beat) – this would lose the surplus half-beat.

In the second bar, a minim rest (two beats) could be substituted for the semibreve rest (four beats). This cuts the total back from six beats to four beats and thus corrects the bar value.

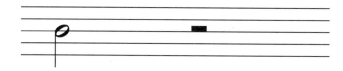

TEST 11 (PAGE 37)

Exercise 1   Refer to CD track 3/6.
Notes: F, E, C, D, E, F, E, D, B♭, C, D, E, F.
Exercise 2   Refer to CD track 3/7.
Notes: G, A, B, C, D, B, E, F♯, G, F, E, D.
Exercise 3   Refer to CD track 3/8.
Notes: F♯, G, G♯, G, G♯, A, F♯.

TEST 12 (PAGE 39)

1. C major.
2. No - it uses B♭.
3. C.
4. Two.
5. No.
6. B.
7. Yes.
8. No, the fourth line.

9. The key is A major. The correct sequence of notes is: A, B, C♯, D, E, F♯ and G♯.
10. G♯.
11. Not necessarily, if you count downward the interval is seven semitones.
12. Four flats.
13. No, this can never happen in any key – the note positions fall on different lines when using different types of clef.
14. Yes – E.
15. No.
16. They have the same pitch but they are not technically the same note.
17. No – the key of C has no sharps.
18. Three.
19. B♭ and E♭.
20. Yes, C and B respectively. As the two keys are a semi-tone apart, ALL of the degrees are also a semitone apart.

TEST 13 (PAGE 46)

1. Four-four.
2. Four-four.
3. Three-four.
4. Three-four.
5. Six-eight.
6. Two-four.
7. Three-four.
8. Two-four.

TEST 14 (PAGE 47)

1. Time signature: Four-four.
   Key: C major.
   Notes: E, G, A, B, A, G, F, G.
2. Time signature: Four-four.
   Key: A major.
   Notes: A, B, C♯, D, E.
3. Time signature: Three-four.
   Key: D major.
   Notes: B.
4. Time signature: Five-four.
   Key: C major.
   Notes: C, D, E, F, E, D, F.
5. Time signature: Twelve-eight.
   Key: F major.
   Notes: F, A, B♭, C, D, E, D, C, B, A.

TEST 14 (CONTINUED)

6. Time signature: Two-four.

   Key: B major.

   Notes: F♯, G♯, A♯, B, G♯.

TEST 15 (PAGE 54)

1. B, F♯, G♯.

2. G, C.

3. F, C♯.

4. B♭, D, F♯.

5. B, D, A♯.

6. B♭, F, E.

TEST 16 (PAGE 55)

1. Natural minor.

2. Melodic minor.

3. Natural minor.

4. Harmonic minor.

5. Melodic minor.

6. Harmonic minor.

7. Natural minor.

8. Melodic AND Natural minor (the two scales are the same when played descending).

TEST 17 (PAGE 59)

1. C-C   (Octave).

2. D-F♯   (Major 3rd).

3. B♭-E♭ (Perfect 4th).

4. E-F♯   (Major 2nd).

5. A-G♯   (Major 7th).

6. F-B♭   (Perfect 4th).

7. C-E   (Major 3rd).

8. C-E   (Major 3rd).

9. D-B   (Major 6th).

10. B-D♯ (Major 3rd).

11. A-F♯ (Major 6th).

12. C-B   (Major 7th).

13. F-D   (Major 6th).

14. G-D   (Perfect 5th).

15. E♭-G (Major 3rd).

16. A-F♯ (Major 6th).

17. F-E   (Major 7th).

18. C-B   (Major 7th).

19. B♭-E♭ (Perfect 4th).

20. E♭-B♭ (Perfect 5th).

21. G-A   (Major 2nd).

22. F-D   (Major 6th).

23. D-C♯   (Major 7th).

24. G-F♯   (Major 7th).

25. A♭-B♭ (Major 2nd).

26. D-D   (Octave).

27. A-C♯   (Major 3rd).

28. G-C   (Perfect 4th).

29. B♭-D   (Major 3rd).

30. E-G♯   (Major 3rd).

31. B♭-E♭ (Perfect 4th).

32. A-G♯   (Augmented 5th).

33. A-G   (Minor 7th).

34. B-C   (Minor 2nd).

35. A-F   (Minor 6th).

36. B-A♯   (Minor 7th).

37. E-A♯   (Augmented 4th).

38. A-F   (Minor 6th).

39. C-A♯   (Augmented 6th).

40. F-A   (Augmented 3rd).

Note that exercises 33 to 40 are set on the bass clef.

TEST 18 (PAGE 60)

1. Perfect 5th (harmonic).

2. Major 2nd (melodic).

3. Minor 7th (harmonic).

4. Major 2nd (harmonic).

5. Perfect 4th (melodic).

6. Major 6th (melodic).

7. Minor 3rd (melodic).

8. Major 7th (harmonic).

9. Minor 3rd (harmonic).

10. Perfect 5th (melodic).

TEST 19 (PAGE 63)

1. Major 2nd.

2. Perfect 5th.

3. Minor 3rd.

4. Minor 6th.

5. Major 7th.

6. Augmented 5th.

7. Diminished 5th.

8. Diminished 2nd.

9. Minor 6th.

10. Perfect 4th.

TEST 19 (CONTINUED)

11. Perfect 5th.
12. Diminished 4th.
13. Augmented 5th.
14. Minor 3rd.
15. Major 6th.
16. Major 2nd.
17. Minor 3rd.
18. Diminished 5th.
19. Augmented 4th.
20. Diminished octave.

TEST 20 (PAGE 64)

1. C–G (Perfect 12th).
2. E–C♯ (Major 13th).
3. B–E♭ (Diminished 11th).
4. G–E (Major 13th).
5. B♭–F (Perfect 12th).
6. F♯–D♯ (Major 13th).
7. A–F (Minor 13th).
8. G–D (Perfect 12th).

TEST 21 (PAGE 67)

1. Transposed to E major.

2. Transposed to A major.

3. Transposed to C major.

4. Transposed to E♭ major.

5. Transposed to D major.

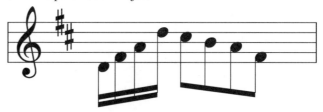

6. Transposed to C major.

7. Transposed to A major.

8. Transposed to D♭ major.

9. Transposed to G major.

10. Transposed to A♭ major.

TEST 22 (PAGE 70)

1. G augmented.
2. D major.
3. F major.
4. A minor.
5. B♭ minor.
6. G major.
7. A diminished.
8. E augmented.

TEST 23 (PAGE 71)

1. Major
2. Minor
3. Diminished
4. Minor
5. Augmented
6. Major.

TEST 24 (PAGE 73)

1. C major, first inversion.
2. C major, open position.
3. E minor, first inversion.
4. A minor, first inversion.
5. D major, first inversion.
6. F major, second inversion.
7. C diminished ,second inversion.
8. C major, open position, second inversion.
9. C augmented, second inversion.
10. B major, second inversion.

TEST 25 (PAGE 75)

1. C major.
2. D major.
3. E minor.
4. A minor.
5. E major.
6. F major.
7. D minor.

TEST 26 (PAGE 76)

1. Dominant seventh
2. Major seventh.
3. Dominant seventh.
4. Minor seventh.
5. Half-diminished seventh.

6. Minor seventh.
7. Major seventh.
8. Half-diminished seventh.

TEST 27 (PAGE 85)

(See staves on the opposite page)

Bar 1

The tied minim and crotchet are replaced by a dotted minim.

Bar 2

The three tied crotchets are replaced by a dotted minim.

Bar 3

The beam of eight quavers must be broken up into a group of four and a group of two (four is the maximum that can be used in a time signature of four-four). The two tied quavers at the end of the beam are replaced by a single crotchet.

Bar 4

No change.

Bar 5

As the four beamed quavers take up the middle two beats of the bar they must be broken up into two pairs to fit in with the beat.

Bar 6

No change.

Bar 7

The tied crotchets are replaced by a minim. Also, in line with standard notation practice, the stems on the beamed quavers would be better shown pointing in the opposite direction.

Bar 8

There is one beat two many in this bar. A number of options exist to correct this fault. The two tied minims could be converted into a semibreve and the crotchet rest thrown away. Alternatively, the final note could be made a dotted minim allowing the crotchet rest to remain in place.

Key Signature

With its six sharps, we can tell immediately that the key signature of the music is F♯ – thus the scale notes are F♯, G♯, A♯, B, C♯, D♯, E♯ and F♯.

Notes

Bar 1 F♯, G♯.

Bar 2 A♯, G♯, A♯.

BAR 1   BAR 2   BAR 3

BAR 4   BAR 5   BAR 6

BAR 7   BAR 8

TEST 27 (CONTINUED)

Bar 3 B, C#, D#, E#, F#, G#, A#.

Bar 4 C#.

Bar 5 B, A#, B, A#, F#.

Bar 6 G#.

Bar 7 B, A#, G#, E#.

Bar 8 F#.

TEST 28 (PAGE 91)

1. Major.

2. Minor pentatonic.

3. Whole-tone/augmented.

4. Major pentatonic.

5. Natural minor.

6. Minor pentatonic.

7. Melodic minor.

8. Harmonic minor.

TEST 29 (PAGE 99)

To aid interpretation the sequence has been divided into repeated sections:

1. A, B, C, D (repeat from start).

2. A, B, C, D (ignore repeat), E, F (repeat from bar E).

3. E, F (ignore repeat) G (repeat from the sign).

4. B, C, D (ignore repeat), E, F (ignore repeat), G (ignore *dal segno*), H (return to *da capo*).

5. A, B, C, D (ignore repeat), E, F (ignore repeat), G (ignore *dal segno*), <u>ignore</u> bar H and play bar I to *fine*.

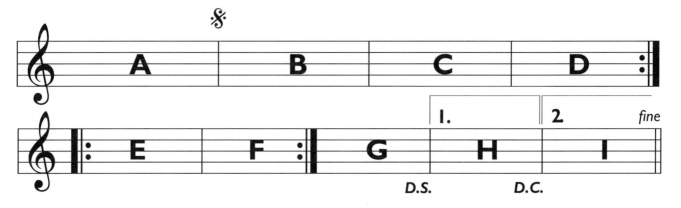

Index

Acknowledgements and bibliography

Terry Burrows would like to thank the following people for their help with this project: Lucian Randall and Zoe Mercer at Carlton books; Hugh Schermuly for his design expertise; Andrew O'Brien for his corrections and suggestions; Aaron King for his Americanizations; Nick Kaçal for dealing with dull queries relating to music theory; and, of course, Junoir.

Derek Bailey – *Improvisation* (Moorland, 1980)

David Bowman and Paul Terry – *Aural Matters* (Schott, 1993)

Terry Burrows – *Total Guitar Tutor* (Carlton, 1998)

Terry Burrows – *Play Rock Guitar* (Dorling Kindersley, 1995)

Terry Burrows – *Play Country Guitar* (Dorling Kindersley, 1995)

Richard Chapman – *The Complete Guitarist* (Dorling Kindersley 1993)

Ralph Denyer – *The Guitar Handbook* (Pan, 1992)

Juan Martín – *El Arte De Flamenco de La Guitarra* (United Music, 1982)

Don Randall – *The New Harvard Dictionary Of Music* (Harvard University Press, 1986)

Darryl Runswick – *Rock, Jazz and Pop Arranging* (Faber and Faber, 1992)

Erik Satie – *A Mammal's Notebook: Collected Writings...* (Atlas, 1996)

Aaron Shearer – *Classic Guitar Technique* (Franco Colombo, 1963)

Nicolas Slonimsky – *Thesaurus of Scales and Melodic Patterns* (Scrivener's, 1947)

Eric Taylor – *The AB Guide to Music Theory* (Associated Board, 1989)

Jason Waldron – *Progressive Classical Guitar* (Koala, 1992)

101 Folk Songs for Buskers (Wise, 1989).